GULISTAN
KHAMZAYEVA

BEHIND
THE SILK
CURTAIN

BEHIND THE SILK CURTAIN

by Gulistan Khamzayeva

© 2022, Gulistan Khamzayeva

© 2022, Glagoslav Publications

Book cover and interior book design by Max Mendor

Cover image: © Aika Alemi (2022)

www.glagoslav.com

ISBN: 978-1-91433-770-3

A catalogue record for this book is available
from the British Library.

This book is in copyright. No part of this publication may be reproduced, stored in a retrieval system or transmitted in any form or by any means without the prior permission in writing of the publisher, nor be otherwise circulated in any form of binding or cover other than that in which it is published without a similar condition, including this condition, being imposed on the subsequent purchaser.

GULISTAN
KHAMZAYEVA

BEHIND THE SILK CURTAIN

GLAGOSLAV PUBLICATIONS

CONTENTS

FOREWORD	8
ACKNOWLEDGMENTS	11
INTRODUCTION	13
CHAPTER I THE BEGINNING	18
CHAPTER II TRANSITORY TERRITORY	28
CHAPTER III CUTTING CULTURAL FETTERS	40
CHAPTER IV GOOD PEOPLE ARE ALWAYS THERE	65
CHAPTER V ON EXPERIENCES AND CHALLENGES	80
CHAPTER VI SPEAKING OF LANGUAGES	108
CHAPTER VII THINKING AND RETHINKING EDUCATION	131
CHAPTER VIII A SENSE OF BELONGING	146
CHAPTER IX VEILS AND FAIRYTALES	162
CHAPTER X CHARITY BEGINS AT HOME	181
EPILOGUE	201
BIBLIOGRAPHY AND SUGGESTED READING	203

*Dedicated to Irene Koch, my best friend,
who made my life complete*

FOREWORD

From 2008 to 2011 I have served in Astana as the European Union Ambassador to Kazakhstan, after previous EU postings — out of Brussels — in Vienna, Kiev, and Moscow and before a final posting in Tashkent, Uzbekistan. In all these postings I was glad that my wife was ready to join me, supporting me in my function as well as allowing us to have a normal family life.

The author's family has in many regards had a similar life to our own and many of the aspects described in this book are not unfamiliar to us. Changing place of work and of living more than once is an exciting experience, and we ourselves consider that we have been privileged to have such an experience, as it allowed us to get a more in-depth knowledge of a number of other cultures and to have made many good friends around the world. There are of course also a number of more or less hard challenges that come along with this, especially as regards family life.

Gulistan Khamzayeva has lived abroad with her family for most of the recent 20 years and it appeared immediately to me that she was indeed very well placed to describe what it means to live abroad and to serve abroad in a diplomatic service. Ambassador Khamzayev is among the senior diplomats of his country and Gulistan Khamzayeva has supported him very actively, getting herself involved in numerous activities.

Gulistan very skillfully describes how she, her husband and their daughters organized their lives in the various places, what special obstacles they had to face and how they faced them. It appears clearly that they have used their new life experiences to enrich themselves and to maintain very close links among themselves, probably closer than if they had stayed in their homeland.

The book provides also the opportunity to learn more about Gulistan's native country, as she refers to Kazakh traditions and as she and her family naturally approach new living environments with their specific cultural background.

Moreover, I would like to underline another aspect that comes to my mind when reading this book: Gulistan and Almaz Khamzayev were diplomats for a country that did not exist when they were born, when they studied, and even when they started their professional career. Indeed, Kazakhstan declared its independence in the context of the disintegration of the Soviet Union only on 16 December 1992. As a new country, Kazakhstan undertook to create all the structures that go along with an independent country. This included the creation of a Ministry of Foreign Affairs and of a diplomatic service. Under the active leadership of President Nazarbayev, Kazakhstan's diplomatic service unfolded gradually over the last 20 years, leading as of now to an impressive network of more than 60 diplomatic missions abroad.

The book at hand is interesting for all those who have lived abroad or who are considering going abroad, as well as for those who are interested in historic elements related to Kazakhstan's nation building.

Finally, the book gave me the opportunity to renew contact with Central Asia, a region that both myself and my wife enormously appreciate. I would encourage you to use this book as a mean to get to know Kazakhstan and its friendly people before possibly travelling there. I can assure you, you will not be disappointed.

Norbert Jousten
EU Ambassador to Kazakhstan
2008-2011April 2013

ACKNOWLEDGMENTS

When my first book, *Leaving a Piece of My Heart Behind*, was published in Russian in 2009, my foreign friends, unable to read in Russian, asked me to translate the book. I told them that it was written for my country people, for the Russian-speaking community, for the people with the same background.

It is about women who due to their husbands' job had to leave the home country to follow their husbands, to find their own way in the host country, to adapt, socialize and accept a new environment. I received lots of warm feedback, comments, and messages, and I am still receiving them.

I promised my foreign friends that one day I will write a book for them to know more about us, Kazakhstani people, to get to know about our culture, some of our traditions, way of living, about our perception of the world around us, globalized and fast moving.

I would like to thank, first of all, my family for supporting me with this project. Otherwise, I wouldn't even start it.

I am grateful to my husband Almaz for still accepting my ideas as I always have lots of ideas and for "pushing" me to take more challenges. Thanks to him I am what

I am. Thirty-six years of marriage help us understand each other in a more profound way, leaving no doubt about the sincerity of our relationship.

My daughters are my friends, my supporters, my counselors. They urged me to write my first book, and they strongly support me in writing this book, giving their contribution, advice, and comments. Mother's thanks to my daughters!

Special thanks to David for editing my book, for the excellence he brought to the book. Besides his infinite amount of patience with my book, I want to thank him for his wisdom, impeccable sense of humor, and creativity with the book cover.

I want to mention and thank Irina Shestakova (wife of Ambassador of Belarus to the Italian Republic) and Irene Koch for their support, encouragement and invaluable comments on how to improve the book.

Last but not least, I would like to thank Catharina Creysel for igniting the idea of this book in me. At some point of writing, we both realized that two books are better than one, and I look forward to reading her inspiring ideas in a book of her own.

INTRODUCTION

We were sitting in the terrace one evening. "It won't be the same in Belgium," I said. "I will miss our garden, this big magnolia tree. I've made so many photos of its flowers! I even painted one on canvas and gave it to Anar because it is her favorite flower. I'll miss my plants, my favorite cactus. Remember? We bought it in the mar- ket in a tiny pot and now it has babies around it like our grandchildren. The cactus and the grandchildren grew up together".

We had come to Italy eight years before, my hus- band and I, with no children. Now there were five of us and the kids were seven years old! Time flies so fast! I worried about them –the new school, new environment, new friends, new languages.

"Our grandchildren will have to switch from speaking Russian to English now," I said.

"I worry about them too," replied my husband. "But our grandchildren are different from their mothers, our daughters. They're mobile, flexible, they'll adapt to a new environment quickly. You'll see."

"I forgot to tell you, Almaz, that Francesco called Ar- lan "*piccolo ambasciatore*". He looks like you –he's a little ambassador." I gazed from the terrace. "It is true. Dayana and Arlan are traditional TCKs!"

"What is that?" he asked, peering into the distance.

"*Third Culture Kids*", I answered. "You know, the book I read".

It was a remarkable book, "Third Culture Kids", written by David C. Pollak and Ruth E. Van Reken, about children growing up in a multi-cultural environment.

The actual term wasn't new, introduced in the early 1950s by sociologist/anthropologist Ruth Hill Useem, who studied children exposed to different societies. But this recent book (the revised version published in 2009) spoke to me and my situation. Thanks to the book I found an exact definition of what my family goes through, what we, our children and grandchildren, are. According to the book, TCKs are kids who are taken into another society when their parents move for occupational reasons. TCKs are also called, as in our case, "little ambassadors", or "kids of the future", brought up, as the book says, in a highly mobile world.

As for me, I am not a TCK, as I left my country, the Republic of Kazakhstan, for the first time for a long-term post abroad when I was thirty-eight years old. Rather, I am a "cross-cultural adult". This term, according to the book, is for someone who has lived in another society or has had meaningful cross-cultural experiences for an extended time period.

In any case, my home, Kazakhstan, is a multinational country with over 120 ethnicities, living peacefully with each other. The issue of nationality was never raised in our minds when I grew up there or even today. I remember once in school, when I was fourteen, our Russian-language teacher started the class by naming some of us and asking us to stand up. Even after we stood up we didn't understand why she had called on us. Then she said: "Please, tell the class what nationality you are, each of you". It took us half a minute to ponder and then say what nationality we were, as we were not used to saying such a thing, in any situation. Finally the teacher said: "I checked your homework and found that Russians in the class made many more mistakes than non- Russians did". That was the only case when we were considered different. Even at that, I am sure none of us related that case to our nationality as we were part of the Soviet Union and home for many ethnic groups which at different periods of time settled in our country looking for a refuge, to explore the vast territory and its resources, whether willingly or under duress (e.g. under Stalin's regime).

Our daughters, Anar, Asel, and Asem and our grandchildren Dayana and Arlan, are all textbook examples of TCKs. Our daughters left Kazakhstan when two of them were fourteen (twins) and one was eight. Two of them as adults remained in a host culture, forming their own families with their non-Kazakhstani husbands. Our grandchildren were born in Kazakhstan, but when they were two and four months old, we took them to Italy. For several years, they didn't know who they were. Once, when they were asked where they were from, they said they were Italians. When they went to kindergarten at the Russian Embassy, they would say they were Russians. They would even proudly say: "We are Russians, and Russians would die rather than surrender to enemies!" This was a saying they picked up from their Russian playmates. At that point, we realized it was time to talk to our grandchildren and explain who they were.

In our diplomatic circumstance, we lead a nomadic lifestyle moving from one country to another, packing up and settling down in a new place, becoming immersed in a new language, and meeting new challenges. Each country we lived in inspired us to grow in different ways. As for me, I acquired computer skills, and started to drive in the United States. And, most importantly, I gained confidence in my abilities and strength as a person. Great Britain was the shortest posting abroad (less than one year). There, as a teacher of English by profession, I kept myself busy with reading in English and traveling around the beautiful countryside. Spain was the country we all developed a special fondness for. I involved myself in charity and started hobbies. In Madrid, I became a vice president of Damas Diplomaticas (Lady Diplomats), and of the Asian Diplomatic Association. I became an honorary member of an association for disabled children and young adults of Alicante (southeastern Spain) and received an award from the association for my charity work. In Italy I discovered my creative side, painting and writing. And I can definitely say, we left pieces of our hearts everywhere we lived.

Suddenly, we were moving yet again, this time to Belgium. It had been the United States, then Great Britain, then Spain, and then Italy. Our ambassador status has also been accredited for Greece, Malta, San Marino, although we never really lived there, but only visited for business matters. All the postings were for fairly long periods, except for Great Britain. We never considered them to be temporary places to live. When we arrived to each country, we really settled in as though we were staying for good. They say "there is nothing more permanent than the temporary", and I couldn't agree more.

This book is about our multicultural life. It is about us, the lives of our children and grandchildren, about our adaptation to new environments, about cultural differences we experienced, about our nomadic way of life, about people we met in different countries and those who left imprints on our lives, about our worries and feelings, about the joys and challenges, about cross-cultural interactions, about living in various cultural worlds, often simultaneously. These situations have moved me to tell our stories in order to sort out the intricacies of who we are, and to help other people in similar situations to come to grips with who they are. We are not alone, as we live in a globalized world with all its challenges and opportunities. How to deal with this situation is what this book is all about.

CHAPTER I
THE BEGINNING

"All travel has its advantages. If the passen-ger visits better countries, he may learn to improve his own. And if fortune carries him to worse, he may learn to enjoy it."

Samuel Johnson

My husband, Almaz Khamzayev, started his diplomatic career at the Ministry of Foreign Affairs of Kazakhstan after graduating from the University of Foreign Languages in 1977, where we met each other. Later he received his Master's degree at the Diplomatic Academy in Moscow, Russia. He was among the first diplomats of the independent Kazakhstan who opened the first embassy in the United States of America. He started from scratch as Chargé d'Affaires, minister-counselor of the Embassy of Kazakhstan to the US to face new challenges in one of the biggest democratic countries in the world. There was no embassy, no residence to work or live in, no cars, nothing to start from. It took him and his team of just three people about six months to take care of all logistics related to setting up an embassy, i.e. looking into and dealing with the formalities of establishing an office, finding an embassy residence, renting apartments for personnel, buying cars, etc..

When Almaz told us we would be leaving soon, we got excited but at the same time upset because he had to leave for the US earlier than we could. And we didn't realize that it would take almost five months to join him there. I was left with three daughters: teenage twins, Anar and Asel, and the youngest, Asem, who was eight years old. How could we start preparing for a journey abroad?

We chose to start by learning the language. I was an English university teacher in Almaty, the biggest city of Kazakhstan, and the kids were learning German just because we lived close to a specialized German school. I informed the dean of the university where I worked about my departure and he asked me to find a substitute, which I had managed to do. Some time before that, I had been notified by the University of Foreign Languages that I was admitted for a PhD program, which I had been awaiting for several years. It was my last chance because of the age limit and I had to make a choice between staying and doing my degree or joining my husband. For me, it was more important to keep the family together. As for the kids, in their mind, they were already in the States and for that reason had stopped taking their local schooling seriously.

What bothered me most was that everybody began asking me when we were leaving and I couldn't give a definite answer. The Ministry of Foreign Affairs was reluctant to send us off. Then I decided to talk to the minister and get a perspective on what we had to do. Instead of clarifying things, he tried to persuade me not to be in a hurry. He recalled his own posting when he was working alone with no family. It didn't sound convincing to me, though, and I insisted that we should go to the US as soon as possible. It took him two months to consider the issue and finally I was informed that I could take the kids with me, but that the Ministry would pay only for one child.. The dilemma was that we had three children. The twins were inseparable and at the same time I couldn't leave the youngest one, so we were stymied by the decision. Later after another visit to the Ministry they made an exception – allowing us to take twins and leaving the third one in Kazakhstan.

I arrived home upset with the news and when the girls heard the predicament, they kept silent for a while and then the youngest one, Asem, exclaimed: "Mommy, please take the twins with you, they cannot be separated and I will stay here with our relatives. Besides, it is more important for my sisters to study abroad." At that moment I thought it was an adult talking to me, as it sounded too mature for an eight-year-old girl. But Asem was always a bit too mature for her age.

The twins didn't utter a word.

"What are you thinking all about?" I asked. Why don't you say anything?"

"We don't know what to say," they answered. "We want to go, and everybody knows we are leaving. But at the same time we know we can't leave Asem." This was looking like a problem for Solomon to solve.

After talking to Almaz, we decided to buy an airline ticket for Asem ourselves. That was a lot of money for us at that time and I didn't know how to get it. Finally, we managed to borrow money from our friends and we all left together.

Nowadays, young diplomats do not have to choose whether to take their children with them or not. Moreover, they are paid for as many kids as they have. They move with their families from one country to another. Some diplomats take nannies with them to take care of the kids abroad. While the wives can be busy working at the embassy and adapting to the new environment, there is someone else at home to take care of the household and the kids.

There is another tendency emerging in Kazakhstan. Some wives, most often wives of ambassadors, do not accompany their husbands abroad for various reasons: because of the job they have at home, or because they have to take care of elderly parents, or because their grown-up children studying at universities in Kazakhstan need to be looked after. Wives visit their husbands sometimes but usually do not stay with them for long. Each person chooses what is best in that particular case. In this sense, Kazakhstani people are very home and family oriented. Even if the immediate family is small, it is surrounded by the bigger circle of relatives. Besides, interpersonal relationships are more important in our culture. In general, Kazakhs are not as mobile as Americans, for instance.

At that time, however, the only real possibility for us was to uproot the entire family to leave. When the paperwork was done, and we had airline tickets in our hands, we started packing. In 1993 we did not have much to pack; we did not even have proper suitcases as we had hardly moved anywhere except on rare trips to Taraz, where my husband's parents lived. It is five hundred and twenty kilometers from Almaty to Taraz, to the south of the country. We had made another major trip together to Moscow when Almaz graduated from Moscow Diplomatic Academy. We spent five days in Moscow sightseeing. That was a great time spent together before our first posting.

After this, packing became an indispensable part of our life for years. We moved to five countries, making nine major moves from one house to another overseas, and in between we did lots of packing for vacations, business trips, studies, and work, as when Asem moved to Florence after finishing her studies, and Anar went to Brussels to work on her thesis at The Center for European Policy Studies.

When it comes to packing, everybody tries to put it off until the last minute or leave it to the most organized and responsible member of the family (usually this is me) to do it for the whole family. My husband once exclaimed: "I am sick and tired of packing!" In the beginning he did the packing. Actually, he is the best at packing. But he takes a long time because he is so tidy and therefore so slow that it takes all his blood, sweat, and tears to finish the job. So, finally, I decided to take over. Now I can understand him, as I have also gotten fed up with the tiring and boring process of packing. You start putting everything in order, labeling boxes, sorting out things, but finally you put everything into one box and forget to redo the label. Over the years you become overloaded with unnecessary things which later you get rid of, keeping in mind an American proverb: "Someone's trash is someone else's treasure".

Recently, I called my friend Olga Poyarkova, a wife of ambassador of Ukraine to the Italian Republic. She was in the process of packing to leave the country for another posting. Olga was such an easy-goer. She said: "You know, Gulistan, the most unpleasant part of our diplomatic life is packing! But the more problems we have, the younger we are!"

Leaving a familiar environment is always painful, especially when you do it for the first time, so far away. Besides, we did not know what to expect: how long we would be staying, whether we were going to have a vacation, what the weather would be like there, what kind of education our girls could get, etc..

Thanks to Almaz, who left earlier than we did, our adaptation was mercifully smooth. He made our living as comfortable as he could as he chose the apartment with furniture and made a few adjustments inside. We had a car, and we did a lot of travelling as there was so much to see and explore. Besides, Almaz collected half of a year's salary to spend on us, which we did successfully on the first days of our arrival to Washington, D.C..

Excitement usually starts when a family discusses a future trip. In our case, this meant realizing how long the distance was between Kazakhstan and the US (over 6550 miles from Almaty to Washington D.C., or about thirteen and a half flight hours), determining what airline to take, deciding what to be busy with during the flight (a very long-distance flight), and so forth. Such discussions, especially for children, are very important. We adults do not treasure the details, and they are not always the same and maybe not as important for us as for children, and I am sure they will do the same thing when they have their own kids. On the eve of our departure to Brussels, our seven-year-old grandchildren didn't sleep well, they were so excited! They had their own little trolleys with lots of "handy" things inside. And all the way to our destination they were asking us nonstop questions about a new place. Kids remember selectively but this trip our grandchildren will never forget.

Pre-departure excitement overwhelmed us. The talks were only about the future trip to that far-away part of the world. Our neighbors, relatives, school teachers, and classmates paid visits to say good-bye.

The last night before leaving was a sleepless one for all of us: Anar, Asel, and Asem, and me. Of course, we did not know that we would come back in four years with no vacation in between.

We moved to the US in February 1993. We made the transit stop in Moscow covered with snow, where we stayed for one night at the hotel and then took a flight to Ireland and finally to Washington, D.C.. That was the first long-distance trip we had ever made and that's why we remember it in detail. Now I can imagine what first impression Americans, people used to a high quality of life and options to choose from, had when they moved to Kazakhstan. The word "choice" impressed us greatly in the USA. We have never realized before what it could mean. Actually we were not given choices during Soviet times. This new situation engulfed us: *You have a choice to make! Sounds great! When you are given a choice, you are given freedom.*

Once, in Spain, I was asked by a Canadian friend to talk to a young American woman who was going to go to Kazakhstan because of her husband's job as a diplomat. We met in the Spanish cafeteria called "Embassy" (we didn't choose the name of the cafeteria on purpose; it was one of the popular places in Madrid to meet people). She brought a thick folder given by her embassy and compiled by the US State Department. I asked her if I could quickly look through it. Now I regret I couldn't ask her to lend it to me for a couple of days so that I could read through it, since, on the basis of this folder we could have compiled our own manual to be used by our people — a task I later accomplished using other sources in Madrid. In any case, since she had read the manual and knew the general information about Ka- zakhstan, I asked her if she had specific questions for me. The first question struck me: "Is it safe to jog in Kazakhstan?" I was surprised by her question, because I would have asked, let's say, about the trans- port, weather, supermarkets and stores, dry cleaning or money changing. But her question was about jog- ging. Later I thought that perhaps she knew everything there was to know about Kazakhstan, except about the first vital thing she would do after settling down in my country: jogging. I am sure Kazakhstan was considered to be a hardship posting, especially at the beginning of our independence. On the other hand, I understand how helpful it might be for a foreigner to go to a new place with adequate knowledge about the country.

Entry always takes time. Newcomers, whether they are prepared for the move or not, need time to adjust, to sniff out the country, so to speak. After the first days of excitement pass, and we need to get on with reality: open a new bank account, wait for an ID card to be issued, fill in the papers for medical insurance, and other paper work.

I remembered one incident we had in Madrid: our driver had trouble getting money from a cash machine. In Kazakhstan they had only just started installing cash machines when we left. Before, people used to get their salary in cash, and there were no credit or debit cards at first. Besides, cash machines in Spain were operated in Spanish, except in the very center of Madrid. On this occasion, the driver couldn't read Spanish and was too shy to ask for help from the people of our embassy. When I realized what the problem was, I willingly showed him how to use a cash machine.

Years later, I myself had a trouble getting money from a cash machine the first days in Rome. I couldn't recognize the word "cash withdrawal". All instructions were given in Italian. That term had no English cognate: "prelievo". I entered a bank and addressed people there in English, but nobody knew English, except one client who just came in. In a foreign country, sometimes the simplest things are the ones that give you the most trouble.

At that time, I realized we needed to compile our own manual for the newcomers and I did it with the help of the embassy personnel. In London I also composed a detailed manual for our people with prices and timetables, sightseeing routes, and practical vocabulary. There were lots of manuals that other embassies had prepared for their own people but we needed our own version, written in our language to help our people understand the new ways and adjust to the new surroundings.

I also worked as a receptionist at our embassy in London and my workday usually started with sorting out and dealing with daily situations, such as calling schools or kindergartens and speaking to principles or teachers at the request of our mothers who spoke no English, talking to doctors to get appointments, calling pharmacies to ask for particular drops or tablets.

Now, reflecting on our first trip to the United States, I can definitely say that we were completely unprepared for the first posting. The same thing happened when we moved to Spain in 1999. No information, no embassy, no people to help with adjusting to the new environment. That's why they were the toughest of all the postings we had over the last nineteen years abroad.

Now I know what to expect. I now view our postings as another adjustment to the Italian, or Belgian system–thinking local and getting things done as efficiently as possible. My experiences have informed my views on life outside my country.

CHAPTER II

TRANSITORY TERRITORY

"...the greatest reward and luxury of travel is to be able to experience everyday things as if for the first time, to be in a position in which almost nothing is so familiar it is taken for granted"

Bill Bryson

Transition is different for everyone. If you move overseas for the first time, it is one thing, but if you make constant moves, it is another kind of experience. You can get used to the nomadic way of living, where every territory is transitory. Everyone in the family makes the transition at different stages and paces. The settling-in stage can also last differently, ranging from a few weeks to a few months.

Practically all parents seek the same kind of information on arriving in a new country: what school to place your kids in, what doctors to see, where to go shopping, what places of interest to visit first, where to get a haircut, where to get a manicure-pedicure, what language courses to sign up for, where to meet a friend for a drink, etc..

When we moved from Washington, D.C. to London directly, we took a hairdryer, an iron, electric toothbrushes, sheets, pillow cases, and bed covers, and all of them were useless because American electric appliances worked on 110 volts instead of 220 in England, and the plugs took plugs with two prongs instead of three, and beds had different dimensions in England. Now you can find appropriate adaptors practically anywhere, but in early 90's they were difficult to find, even in London.

Usually it is the mother's duties to take care of home supplies, look for drapes and carpets, sheets and bed covers, toothbrushes and shampoo, find a hairdresser and the cleaners — in short to make lots of home- settling arrangements for the whole family. Forget about sexist stereotypes; that's just the way it is. In general, women are capable of doing several things at one time. Usually husbands, absorbed in the new job, lose interest in searching for appropriate colors and dimensions, and kids have no interest in anything except for toys if they are small and clothes if they are teenagers.

For my husband and the three girls the change of environment from Kazakhstan to the USA was not traumatic, as they got into the flow of everyday activities immediately. Almaz started his job as a minister- counselor at our embassy in the US with people from our country using their own language, talking to our officials in Kazakhstan, dealing with familiar matters they used to work on. As for the girls, they entered schools in the middle of the school year and were soon involved in school activities, making friends, and socializing. I realized that the smaller the kids were, the easier the adaptation process was. It took two months for Asem, our eight-year-old daughter, to learn English. After a short while, to my delight, I felt that I didn't have to worry about her, as far as the language was concerned. She had learned to make herself understood.

It took our twin daughters half a year to become "Americans", so to speak. They preferred to be together rather than hang around with friends from school. Looking at our twins, I thought that they didn't even need friends, as they felt so comfortable in each other's company. However, the sense of "Americanism" penetrated their mode of behaving anyway: always wearing baggy jeans and T-shirts, sneakers (no heels). In this way they were expressing their idea of freedom.

I would ask them: "Would you like to go out with us?"

"No", they would often reply, "we have the right to choose, and we choose to stay at home and listen to the music." That was their usual answer.

Once, while talking about the kids to my friend Benedikte Bernhard, wife of the ambassador of Denmark in Spain, I remarked that the girls were reluctant to go sightseeing. She said: "You know, Gulistan, we have the same situation with our son. I think, they realize that they will have so much to see in future, that they are not in a hurry now. As for us, it might be the last chance to see this or that place." Benedikte was right. With the passing of time, our twins have admitted that they missed seeing many things around the States, and they recalled having behaved a bit silly a times. For example, when they were given a choice of foreign languages to learn at school, they chose Russian as a foreign language. We shamed them for that. In reply, they justified their choice: "Mom, they do not know we speak Russian. They do not expect it from us; we look Asian to them." The next day they changed their minds and chose French as a foreign language. And I thought that there were always two sides to a coin: while having freedom, children need guidance.

As soon as we arrived in Washington, D.C., I started working at our embassy as a receptionist. I didn't want to stay at home all the time feeling lonely and wanted to be useful, since I knew English. While on the job, I received lots of calls from Americans. Many of the callers were peculiar and always friendly, and I could even feel through the receiver how Americans smile when they talk. I guess they do it unconsciously as it is a huge part of their character. Americans are curious about everything that's unknown to them. It is not surprising that they were the first to invest in our country. Their enquiries were sometimes a bit naïve, as they would ask, for example, if the camels are the only mode of transport in Kazakhstan.

I took my job responsibilities seriously as I have always done no matter what was involved. I started compiling English-Kazakh vocabulary, sorted out all the information regarding Kazakhstan we had at that time, since there was nothing we could offer at the beginning of 1993 after the collapse of the USSR. Later we had the information about Kazakhstan not only in English but almost in all other major languages. Now we have more than sixty embassies and foreign missions abroad.

My life outside the embassy at the beginning was not so exciting. I had not made many friends yet. I had not even seen our neighbors, as if they didn't exist. And I could not even call home to Kazakhstan, because it was so expensive. I could only go shopping for hours and come back with no purchase, as I was not in a mood to buy anything. They say that women, coming from thousands of years of nomadic gatherers, are genetically wired to gather things in shops. Maybe that is true.

Everybody knows I love shopping. I do it when I am mad at somebody, at something, or even at myself, to change my mood. I shop when I am sick to feel well, when I have to think over something, when I am looking for a just the right gift. I like going shopping with my husband –he is so generous! They say men come from thousands of years of hunting, and they think of shopping only in terms of efficiency. He does not look at prices; he throws the spear and takes his prey immediately. Actually, he is calm, gentle, and helpful. He loves everything we choose, and he almost never says "no". This is exactly what irritates our youngest daughter, Asem, however. She wants him to be more specific about the color and quality of the clothes she puts on. As for me, I take care to examine the lining, color, composition of the material, usefulness, durability, softness, and so on and so forth. And all of this measured against the price. "Women know best about clothes, children, and education," I heard once. I cannot argue with this. We women are all experts on these things.

As for shopping in general, I would like to give my opinion on where shopping is the best. In Italy! Not because Italy is famous for its fashion brands. No, no. Like everything in Italy, shopping is a fine art. In Italy shopping is relaxing, and enjoyable. If you shop at least twice in the same store, you become a friend of a shop assistant. You will be offered coffee, your purchase will be nicely wrapped, you will receive information on your cell phone about discounts and new arrivals. When Italians go shopping, they usually appreciate what they see: "*Guarda, Mario, que bello!*" ("Look, Mario, how beautiful it is!"). My daughter and I were shopping once in Milan, Italy, the Mecca of shopping. It was a sales time. We were in the boutique when a Russian couple entered the same store and the lady said, with some disdain: "Oh, they still have sales, let's get out of here!" If you are *nouveau riche* and are aching to show off your money, you don't want anybody to think you came for the sales.

Shopping also mixes you in among other people if you are alone, and at the beginning of any move to a new country, there are moments of feeling alone, as in the case of not knowing my neighbors at first in Washington D.C.. But, then again, I have never had difficulty making friends. Over the years, when moving from one country to another, I receive lots of good wishes. I have a thick, lined notebook where I keep those wishes as a memory at different postings. The common remark I get from the people I know is: "I am sure, you will make friends on the spot." "You will be surrounded by friends." "It is no problem for you to make friends," etc.. It is true. I am lucky to have friends from all over the world. I have friends in the US, England, Spain, Italy, Belgium, Germany, Japan, Switzerland, Austria, Uzbekistan, Armenia, Russia, France, Lithuania, Norway, Azerbaijan, Jordan, Malaysia, Thailand, Ukraine, and Belarus. Not to mention Kazakhstan. One of my Spanish friends told me once: "*Mi casa es tu casa!*" ("My home is your home!"). Imagine how many homes I have.

Still, I had that feeling of unsettledness in the United States for a long time as if we had to move away soon, to get back to the family environment, to the home we had left behind back in Kazakhstan. I knew it was a temporary move but I didn't know how long we would stay. The duration wasn't scheduled. This feeling of uncertainty was weighing on me. It seemed to bring out my sense of insecurity. I must admit that I have always felt insecure and self-doubting. I have always thought that somebody else knew better than I did, was wiser than I was, more capable. Maybe it's not surprising that, in the midst of this move to the new, complicated diplomatic world in the vast United States, I lost self-confidence. At times, I was not sure whether I did something right, whether I replied correctly, whether I used the right words, whether I was understood, and so on. The kids were too young to talk to about adult matters, and Almaz had his hands full; I had no friends around. I intended to call my sisters in Kazakhstan but they thought we were happy in America. Would they understand my feelings? They had to cope with daily problems, which I generally didn't face in the States. They didn't need my problems, and probably could not empathize with them. I felt miserable, sorry for myself, and frequently ended up crying. It didn't help and at that moment I realized I needed to release my emotions by putting them on paper. Writing helped me to get over emotional distress. Over time, however, I began to write less as I became more confident and wiser.

As for writing diaries, I have always been skeptical and even thought that only lonely people tend to write them or it is done to keep the memory of the event with the danger of living in the past. Writing about feelings can help the brain overcome emotional upsets and leave your feeling happier, psychologists have found. Brain scans on volunteers have shown that putting feelings down on paper reduces activity in a part of the brain which is responsible for controlling the intensity of our emotions. In part, it bears out the affirmation of D. H. Lawrence: "One sheds one's sicknesses in books –repeats and presents again one's emotions, to be master of them." In my case, I think it was a way of communicating with neighbors I haven't ever seen, with future friends, with my daughters who were too small to have mother-daughter talks, and with Almaz, who didn't like these kinds of irrelevant chats. I didn't keep those scribblings (as I regarded them); they were really insignificant. But they helped me at the beginning to put my thoughts in order to help myself.

As we have daughters, raising them was not easy, especially when they were in their teens. In our Kazakh culture, there is a saying: "When a man has three daughters he can automatically go to heaven no matter what he does in life." It's not clear whether this means that daughters are so difficult that he has earned heaven by dealing with them, or whether having so many daughters is a blessing directly from heaven. In our case, we definitely feel blessed to have three daughters, and each of them is unique, but there is much to worry about when it comes to raising girls. All the changes we went through had an impact on our daughters, too. There was a time when they resisted the rules set in the house, after moving from one country to another, longing for the familiar environment back in Kazakhstan. There were personal issues regarding their appearance: for example, our daughters Anar and Asel were concerned with being overweight during their teenage years. Right before leaving for the US, they had to quit a professional volleyball-training school, which they had attended for seven years. They changed their mode of living, which caused weight problems. The constant change of schools took its toll. Since the circle of communication is limited, kids often turn their anger against the parents, regardless of the real reason for the anger.

Back home in Kazakhstan, it might have been easier for them by talking to their aunts, friends, cousins, as they were used to doing before. Abroad, they felt isolated and could not express themselves openly enough to discuss their problems. Often, especially in the US, it is common to visit family therapists or, as they are often called, "shrinks", and discuss family problems candidly, face to face with your children or spouse in front of a psychologist. We never went through such therapy, but I think it would have been very helpful. Perhaps our problems would have "shrunk".

I came across one of the myriad bits of folk wisdom circulating in cyberspace, called "The Images of Mother" which, with its humor and grain of truth, in fact helped me to see who we are for our daughters at different phases of their growth:

4 years old – My mom can do anything! 8 years old – My mom knows a lot!
12 years old – My mom doesn't really know quite everything.
14 years old – Naturally, mother doesn't know that, either.
16 years old – Mother? She's hopelessly old-fashioned.
18 years old – That old woman? She is way out of date!
25 years old – Well, she might know a little bit about it. 35 years old – Before we decide, let's get mom's opinion.
45 years old – Wonder what mom would have thought about it.
65 years old – Wish I could talk it over with mom.

My daughters had a great impact on me, too. Thanks to them I began following the latest fashion trends, and thanks to their encouragement I lost weight and dramatically changed my wardrobe, tried radical nail colors, and became more confident. I don't know who I would be if I had had sons. My daughters are also my friends and there are no secrets between us. Well…at least none that matter.

When we were in Italy, one Italian *signora* called me "*Bellissima e forte!*"(beautiful and strong). I became strong abroad, constantly facing challenges and overcoming difficulties. No one believes now that I was insecure, that I always underestimated my abilities. Could it be that I matured and I am getting older?

I still miss a lot of things back in Kazakhstan. I miss my job of teaching English, I miss my friends in Kazakhstan, I miss my sisters, I miss spontaneous contact with them, and I miss the events in the lives of people close to me. I even miss our two-storey apartment, which was comfortable and full of fond memories, though we live in more impressive housing now, in big ambassadorial residences.

I came to understand that while reflecting on the past and worrying about the future we live in the present, which poses daily problems that we have to live through. I learned the main "don't": Don't postpone problem solving for the future, when the posting ends; solve it now! My favorite proverb is "Never put off till tomorrow what you can do today", which I have often told my children. They often reply that they will think about that later.

Being a foreign diplomat is an advantage and responsibility. A diplomat has a diplomatic immunity which protects the channels of diplomatic communication by exempting diplomats from local jurisdiction so that they can perform their duties with freedom, independence, and security. Diplomatic immunity is not meant to benefit individuals personally; it is meant to ensure that foreign officials can do their jobs. Representing your own country is a responsibility. Being a diplomat in a foreign country is a double responsibility as people tend to see you as a representative of your country and imagine you as such.

On a personal level, for me the geopolitical map has come to seem an artificial construct laid over a world teeming with natural diversity, including humans. Mountains and trees and rocks are no more Spanish or French or German than is the sky with its clouds and wind. People are people, first and foremost, only afterwards political entities. Yet cultures even at the local level differ. It is a reflection of biodiversity, which reaches to the core of life as an endless source of fascination and awe rather than distress or conflict. Being a foreigner is an opportunity to enjoy diversity, rich tapestry of the world, respect the differences among people, and live affirmatively.

In what seemed like tornado that ripped up our family and sent us whirling abroad, we went through a transition period of personal frustration and disenchantment with the new environment, excitement and expectations, adjusting to and accepting the transitory territory around us. It was our way of overcoming culture shock. We were warned about culture shock. But unless you go through it, for all you hear about it, you don't truly know what it is. There is an old joke:

"How can you take an Irishman by surprise?" "Give him advanced warning."

With culture shock, we are all Irishmen. You can have advanced warning, but it still takes you by surprise.

CHAPTER III
CUTTING CULTURAL FETTERS

"The first condition of understanding foreign country is to smell it."

Rudyard Kipling

When you move to a new country, you get interested in everything, and you notice pretty quickly that things are different. You watch and absorb, smell and taste, listen and feel, and everything seems to be different from what you have in your own country.

Culture is not what we see on the surface but what we evaluate, accept or do not accept, believe, assume, stereotype, generalize, etc.. We all have different ways of looking at things. What seems acceptable in one culture might be unacceptable in another and ignoring this or that matter might cause trouble. Observation, adjustment, and acceptance offer a smoother way to adapt to the new environment.

Our experience in the United States, particularly the first impressions revealed the many cultural differences. When we stepped down from the plane in Washington,

D.C., a four-year-old Kazakh girl, a daughter of one of our embassy personnel, exclaimed:

"Look! That guy is a Negro!"

Her mom put her hand on her daughter's mouth saying: "Don't shout!"

It was a matter of volume for her mom rather than the content of the exclamation. Later they learnt that black people in the US were called "Afro-Americans", or simply "blacks".

In everyday life, the abundance and variety of produce in the US amazed us. By contrast, in Kazakhstan the early 1990s were marked by the absence of basic goods with the lines of people for food and clothes. This situation came right after the collapse of the Soviet Union when each republic of the former USSR was left to take care of itself, managing its own economy. The introduction of a market economy in these countries without a suitable transition was a terrible shock, plunging the different countries into financial ruin far more devastating than the Great Depression in the U.S. after the crash of 1929. All sectors of society felt the dramatic cutbacks in health and education, as well as in other social programs. Poverty spread and the future became a threatening question mark.

We are often asked how we had lived in the Soviet times for seventy-four years prior to our independence. Frankly, life was not all that bad, as a frugal life was balanced with a certain sense of security. By contrast, there was so much precious and positive that was lost after each republic of the Soviet Union acquired its own independence. Big families had been fostered and supported by the government and trade unions. Education and medicine were for free. I remember that, when I was young, children were usually sent to summer camps on the outskirts of the city for three months for free and that was a big help for our parents, especially for those who had four to six kids. It was safe and healthy, and we had fun. The relationship between people was sincere, open and trustworthy. The doors were, in fact, open to anyone. Everybody cared for everything. Everyone simply cared. At least that was the feeling of those years.

In those times, our kids didn't know what bananas looked like, let alone ever tasted one. An orange was presented at the New Year school parties in a pack of sweets as it was a rare fruit. But there were lots of other things which made us happy, such as the opportunity to have fun in the yard for hours playing hide and seek, or to eat watermelon at one of the homes of our classmates or neighbors, while the parents didn't have to worry about kids disappearing, as it was safe and the children were surrounded by individuals who cared what happened to each other and would always offer help.

During the first days in Washington, D.C. our children ate so many oranges and bananas that they became allergic to them. In supermarkets the kids would be stuck in front of the shelves with fifty different kinds of cereal and we, adults, would note other differences such as free museums, good public transport, law- abiding and friendly drivers, huge shopping malls with plenty of movie theatres, ubiquitous garage and yard sales, abundance of air conditioning, a wide variety of restaurants, the absence of hot tea, excess of ice in cold drinks, and much more.

When our youngest daughter Asem invited her American classmates to her birthday party to our house, we were surprised at the beginning when they didn't take their shoes off before entering the house, and they were very selective about their drinks, and were cautious when offered an unusual food. I prepared a lot of Kazakh food for them but they did not touch it at all. The next year, I bought a birthday cake, soft drinks, and sandwiches for her friends and everybody was happy.

One evening we were watching an American movie about the anorexic girl whose parents were forcing her to eat. They didn't actually force her but rather were worried about her. In return, she decided to sue them for what they did. The court received her appeal, and subpoenaed the parents. Then the elder sister tried to dissuade the younger sister from pressing charges. Finally the girl realized that her parents had been acting in her own interest and she dropped the case. That movie was a rude culture shock for us. In our culture, parents are treated with respect. They are often addressed in a formal and respectful way, like *Sie* in German, *Vous* in French, or *Usted* in Spanish. And the word of the parents is final in most families. Even sons- and daughters-in-law are not on a first-name basis with their parents-in-law but rather use the terms "mother" and "father". To address elders, even those who are only two or three years older, and the first and middle names (patronymic, father's name) are used together to show respect for position, seniority, or age. When addressing a guest or an elder, a Kazakh may use a shortened form of the name and the suffix 'ke'. For example, Almaz could be called *Aleke*, my name could be changed from Gulistan to *Guleke*. This should be regarded as indicating a high level of respect for a guest or elder. As a reflection of my exposure to many new customs, my Austrian son-in-law Markus calls me by my first name, and this is not disturbing to me. He is not from Kazakhstan and I don't want to change his ways or impose mine. I know from the way he treats me, his actions, that he respects me as I do him, and that is enough for both of us. Our mutual respect for one another transcends any cultural differences we may have.

Another element which I, as a mother, found to be a cultural difference in the US, is the fact that parents and children are not as close to each other as they are in the culture of Kazakhstan. In the US, as soon as children leave the house to start their own life, they take care of themselves. They virtually start from scratch, supporting themselves financially and making decisions on their own. By contrast, the first time we ever permitted our twins, Anar and Asel, to live by themselves was back in 1999 in London to study towards their BA degree. At first, they were excited about having the freedom to do what they liked without being supervised by their parents anymore. But then, after a few weeks, they began to miss us and call us almost every day. I was on the verge of leaving for London to rescue them, but as the time passed Anar and Asel stopped acting childish and began to come to terms with reality. Later, we found out that this maturity was greatly encouraged by their classmates (a couple of girls from US, a girl from Nigeria, classmates from all over the world going to London to study) who were all on their own without parental supervision. We still support them financially and emotionally, and they share their concerns, and they ask for our advice and make decisions only after consulting us first. It is the physical separation that was such a new experience for all of us. I think this is happening now more and more with modern-day Kazakhs. They and their kids travel more, see more, experience more, and so the physical manifestations of tradition, such as children being with their parents until they get married or even after- wards, dwindle and disappear. However, this does not mean that their children seek less help or advice or guidance from their parents. In some cases, that need is greater because of the distance between the children and parents.

In our culture, parents pamper their children even into their 30s or 40s. The youngest one, especially if it is a young man, lives with his parents and, if he gets married, he brings his wife to his parents' house. In this case, even if he has sisters and brothers who do not live with parents, he inherits everything his parents leave after their death. We actually do not have nursing homes.

In Italy and Kazakhstan the words *casa* and *yù* signify the same, "home", but transmit a broader meaning, of *family* and *hearth*. The Kazakh emblem depicts a roof of the house as a symbol of family and state unity. In Italy the bond between a husband and wife, between two families, between kids and parents, the attitude to kids remind me of my own culture. Kids in Italy are pampered and adored; in fact, we didn't see kids being reprimanded in public even if they behaved badly. Italian men are also pampered by their mothers, being mama's boys, called *mammoni*. Men in Kazakhstan are treated the same by their mothers.

Kazakhstan tradition is, above all, hospitality. Kazakhs never let their guest go without having meals, and it is evidence of generosity and hospitality of our nation. Kazakhs always keep the most delicious food for guests. An occasional guest is called "a guest from God". Once, we were invited to one man's house when I was six years. My father was treated as the most honored man in that house. When it was time to leave, the host invited me to choose anything I liked in his house as a sign of respect towards my father. My mother whispered me to take a carpet she liked, other guests were offering more precious things in the house, and even the host pointed his finger to a horse outside the window. I made a sigh and chose a small iron toy.

During the first years of our independence, when food stores were almost empty, refrigerators in each family were full of food. People got used to stocking up on supplies of meat, vegetables, rice, sugar, flour. I remember my childhood especially during summer. We used to buy sacks of onions, carrots, sugar, flour, and potatoes for winter because of the tradition and a way of living. People preferred to make preserves and store food in their balconies, storage rooms, and garage. I remember my childhood through the sweet smell of compotes and preserves of raspberry, strawberry, black and red currant, apricots, and other fruits. The most experienced women would make preserves out of rose petals, watermelon, apples, for example. All the windows were open as everyone cooked and the smell made you crazy. No wonder, being away from our country, we miss home-made preserves. Even bio preserves abroad do not have the intense flavors and fragrances of those in Kazakhstan.

When I asked my son-in-law Markus after his visit to Kazakhstan, what the trip meant to him, he said, in one word: "Food." I would add, "natural food." Everything smells and tastes. Foreigners visiting Kazakhstan might probably know what it means when they are invited "for tea" in my country. It starts with tea, then an appetizer afterwards, and then the main dish followed by another main dish, to end up again with tea. Coffee is not popular. In short, a table is full of food which is called "*dastarkhan*" and one of the popular toasts in Kazakhstan is "let your dastarkhan be as rich as we have today".

Everyday greetings like "Hi! How are you?" is a formality of addressing people abroad. But not in Kazakhstan. "How are you?" invites a story about the family, its members, illnesses, future plans, prices, latest news. While speaking about holidays, money, cars, food, etc. might be considered boastful in Western culture, in Kazakhstan it is normal to speak about everything, even to unknown people.

People usually greet each other by handshaking and kisses. In Kazakhstan handshaking is essential. The elder and respected men by position are greeted with two hands. Hugs are given more than kisses. The greeting culture in other countries is confusing for me: the number of kisses, what cheek to start with (right or left), kiss or hug, who shakes which hand first. They say that the farther south you go, more hugs and kisses than handshakes are exchanged. But in reality, there is mixture: Spaniards and Italians prefer two cheek kisses, the Russians three, Belgians two occasionally if they are from the Walloon part and three if from West Flanders (starting on the left cheek), the English and Americans, none. According to protocol, women offer their hand in greeting first. In practice men sometimes offer hands first and squeeze the woman's hand so tightly that it causes pain, especially if she is wearing a ring. I try not to wear a ring on my right hand to avoid pain.

Kazakhs nowadays observe a remarkable custom, when a feast is arranged in honor of newly arrived neighbors. For Kazakhs, a well-laid table is a symbol of a good neighborhood. The tradition, which existed since the old times, to invite newcomers to a party helped those newcomers to get accustomed to the new surroundings and to get closer to their neighbors more quickly.

I still remember the face of an Englishwoman I met early in the morning in our neighborhood in East Sheen, London where we relocated right after the US. I saw her first. She was crying while carrying her umbrella as it was raining. I felt so sorry for her, she seemed so fragile, and I even wanted to offer her my help. When she suddenly saw me, she quickly stopped sobbing, and made a quick smile. It looked so abnormal, this immediate switch from crying to smiling, that I couldn't reveal any emotion at that moment. I often recall that episode. I thought at that time that it was true when they said: "My home is my castle." She was outside of her castle with her pouring emotions and she considered herself to be too exposed to the public. I also recall our move to the English neighborhood. Nobody approached to greet us, to say "Welcome." The silence lasted for nine months. By Christmas we received a note from the neighbor that they were glad to have us in their area. We had at long last been accepted in the circle of neighbors.

When our twins returned from UK to Kazakhstan, they got excited. They were remembering their childhood, getting in touch with their former classmates, walking the familiar streets, eating food they missed, spending some time with our relatives, and telling them how the life abroad was. It seemed easy enough for the twins to adjust back home; they found themselves comfortable in a familiar environment. They found our people to be caring, and curious about the world outside Kazakhstan.

The dress code is also a part of culture, especially in Kazakhstan. Our people care about their appearance. Kazakhstani women are very fashion conscious, sometimes even extremely *chic*. That's why the way women dress in Kazakhstan often catches a foreigner's attention. Indeed, so much attention is paid to how well the dress fits with your wardrobe, that the way a woman is dressed is often discussed in the workplace, and so women make sure they put on the right nail color that day to match her outfit. It is also a definition of their status: how wealthy, fashionable, and stylish your clothes are. Like Italians' obsession with appearance, *la bella figura*, people in our culture like to show off by putting on expensive clothes and sometimes are really out of place with the choice of wardrobe. When we came back to Kazakhstan from the USA for a short vacation, my mother said my outfit was too modest as I had already adapted to comfortable, not-too-stylish clothes as opposed to the uncomfortable but fashionable way Kazakhstani people were used to dressing. Whenever you see a well-dressed woman with her hair all done up and high-heeled shoes, she is likely to be from a country of the CIS (Commonwealth of Independent States).

I remember our daughter, Asel, would call from Canada when she was doing consulting for a Canadian company for few months and tell us how her colleagues would ask her about her outfits and how they would be surprised to see her with different nail colors during the week. "How many purses did you bring with you on this trip?" someone would ask Asel. The reply was: "Four to match different shoes and to go with different dresses." She rarely heard conversations between women in the workplace discussing clothes, shoes, hats, etc.. Rather, there was talk about the weather, family, and plans for the weekend.

The difference between Western and Kazakhstani way of dressing up is notable. In Kazakhstan, dressing well is valued over comfort. A basic part of dressing is jewelry. Our women like jewelry. The favorite material of Kazakh jewelry is silver. According to Kazakhs, silver has purifying, protective, and magic properties. Jewelry could tell about the social status and territorial origins of a Kazakh woman. Ladies from wealthy families would have a full set of silver jewelry weighing over three kilograms. The nature and quantity of jewelry would be in accordance with a woman's age: simple earrings and bracelets for young girls, and more complex and attractive arrays for elderly women. Jewelry for hair was traditionally very popular. Jingling hair decorations were meant to protect hair as Kazakhs believed that part of a soul inhabits the hair and bells can scare demons away. Such hair decorations can weigh up to a few kilograms and therefore they pulled the hair back, making for good posture and walking. Jewelry ornaments differed from western to eastern, northern to southern Kazakhstan. For example, typical monumental and large-scale forms were peculiar to western Kazakhstan and a variety of gem stones and corals were found more in the south of the country. Adornments served as good luck charms. Kazakh jewelry has been described as masterpieces carrying a living breath of the endless steppes. *Bijouterie* is still not popular. A positive point of Western culture regarding jewelry is the vast variety of choices in a blend of real jewelry with simple *bijouterie*. Women choose whatever they like even if it doesn't suit their outfit. Nowadays we wear jewelry because it is pretty or just because it makes us feel good, and it doesn't matter where we come from. Perhaps there is something lost in ethnic or regional identity, but there is something gained in personal freedom.

In the spirit of play, we were watching the Euro soccer match between Spain and Italy. Before living in Italy, we had been working in Spain for six years. Our grandchildren were born when we moved to Italy and they lived in Italy with us. When we came to the point of deciding who cheered for which team, the grandkids said: "We are for the Italians; we live here and we love Italy!" The adults were for Spain. It didn't matter to us who won the game (by the way, Spaniards became the champions!). More important was the feeling of belonging to the places we lived in.

Observing how people of the same culture interact with each other is the clue to better assimilation into that culture. I always wondered why some people ignore or refuse to accept the rules of behavior in a given country. I was in a group of foreigners in an Arab country. Some of the western women arrived in see-through clothes, almost half naked by that country's standards. That disregard for the customs of the receiving country could be considered rude and even arrogant. On the other hand, it takes very little self-sacrifice to show your regard for the customs of the country being visited and in that way foster the spirit of mutual respect.

When people make comments like "Kazakhs...don't smile much" or "one of the thinnest books in the world could be *Kazakh Charm*", and judge the vast country without adequate experience, it doesn't encourage mutual respect. When we make assumptions and judgments on appearances, we might be wrong. Smiles are sometimes fake, and a smile with a motive can have a negative connotation. If your smile comes from your heart, you will get a return smile, I am sure.

And some people insist they know everything about a country after a relatively short stay. These are often self-confident people. Often so self-confident that they don't know the words "possibly", "it seems to me", "in my opinion", "maybe", "I doubt", etc.. They don't doubt; they are sure, certain, convinced, firm, definite, unswerving, foursquare, without assuming, suggesting, conjecturing, guessing, vacillating. They would make good sales representatives. They could sell refrigerators to the Eskimos. But would you really trust what they say about the Inuit? If you are a foreigner, you cannot judge a country by what you might see in a market place once, or, if you are an ambassador's wife, by what the maid and the driver tell you in the kitchen. Knowing a country takes time, and careful consideration. I read a book by a person who lived in Kazakhstan for only four years and has made sweeping pronouncements on the new oil-rich Kazakhs vs. the Russians, who the writer believes look down on the Kazaks. The appraisal of interethnic relationships is not easy in any country that I can think of. Fragile relationships can easily erupt into conflicts between factions, whether ethnic or religious. Such glib generalities are not useful in our case. Kazakhs and Russians have been living together for seventy-four years and their lives have intermingled for decades, even centuries. Kazakhs are tolerant people in broad terms, and they consider the country's stability to be the most precious thing. During the Second World War, Kazakhs raised orphans from Russia, despite having their own ten children or more. The Russians I have known or known about, on leaving Kazakhstan for a better life in Russia, have sympathy and warmth in their hearts towards Kazakhstan. They miss our land, their Kazakh friends, Kazakh hospitality. Many of those who left returned to Kazakhstan, as they realized they had not cherished all the advantages they had back home. We have Russian friends who left Kazakhstan many years ago. Whenever they call me or write, I feel how deeply they miss our country. They keep cooking popular Kazakh food, they ask those who go for vacation to Kazakhstan to bring back this or that thing dear to their heart. And they often visit the country to meet their friends, neighbors and to see how developed the infrastructure is nowadays in Kazakhstan. Recently, friends of ours who live in the Moscow region returned from Kazakhstan where they were on vacation with *saksaul*-packed in boxes. Saksaul is a tree that can be found in some desert regions of Central Asia. The trees have very small, soft green needles (which are succulent) and a grey, white or brown bark. The bark can be pressed to extract water since it has a high moisture content. In fact, camels and other animals eat the bark and needles as a source of water. Once the trees are considered dead, the wood is dried and used for fuel. Traditionally, in Kazakhstan saksaul is also used for barbecues because it burns well. We believe that because of saksaul our barbecues are excellent.

The first months we moved to Belgium we met a lovely couple, the European Union Ambassador to Uzbekistan and his wife, Renée Jousten-Janssen, Belgians. Before Uzbekistan they have been working in Kazakhstan for a long time. They have a lot more complex and balanced things to say about the country and they found our winter to be fresh and not harsh, our people friendly and not closed, our country stable and prosperous, not stagnant. As the children's song says, some see the doughnut, some the hole.

In general, Kazakhstan is a little-known country, particularly for Westerners. To begin with, foreigners often mistake the terms "Kazakh" and "Kazakhstani", while the former refers to a person of Kazakh nationality, the latter means a person having Kazakhstan citizenship but being of different ethnic origin, as there are more than a hundred and twenty ethnicities living in Kazakhstan. When our daughter Asel started working for a national company in Kazakhstan, she often interacted with foreign companies doing business in our country. There was an instance she told me about, when, during negotiations a foreigner turned to her to ask why they would refer to someone as being Kazakh and mention others as Kazakhstani. He didn't see the difference until she explained that she considered herself to be both Kazakh and Kazakhstani in origin, having Kazakh roots and being a citizen of Kazakhstan.

When we arrived in the US, our kids would ask us why we didn't celebrate Christmas. As I was explaining "why", I was thinking "why not?" I explained to our children that a majority of Kazakhs were Muslims, but religious feelings were not expressed fervently; the country was peaceful and open-minded towards religion in general, and in our case we didn't even follow religious practice. That's why we were free to celebrate any event, regardless of its faith of origin. Ever since, I got an advent calendar for our grandchildren. It was fun to have candies and little toys hidden in the pockets. When our grandkids were four, we used the calendar to teach them counting as they were looking for a certain date to get candy. What we adults consider work can be made child's play. An advent calendar for our kids means a bright holiday of joy and play.

Recently, on September 22, 2012, a different kind of celebration appeared on Euronews, where we watched people in Marden, Kent, UK having fun by throwing dough at each other. My immediate reaction was that it might be fun throwing mud but not dough, as it is food and we teach our kids not to play with food or waste it. On a more humanitarian level, when there are still millions of people throughout the world who don't have enough to eat, throwing food at each other is a wasteful display, and perhaps one of the worst sides of needless consumerism. It seems to overlook the old British saying: "Bread is the staff of life."

In Kazakhstan, bread is always in the centre of the table. Guests will be served tea and bread, even if they are not invited to a meal. In my country bread is sacred; it is cheap but sacred. You would never see people stepping on bread as this would be a sin to us. People would pick it up with their hands and put it aside or collect it to feed animals. We were never deprived of bread even during the Second World War, but it is a tradition to touch it when you want somebody to believe you or to swear, or taste it to show respect. There is a tradition to take leftovers from the table, especially from the holiday *dastarkhan* for children and grandchildren. The meaning of this tradition is to treat food with respect and bring joy to family members. There are many more things that people can have in common; there are simple, everyday things which should remain sacred, things that we should cherish.

In Italy, I was invited to the presentation of a book about bread entitled *The Civilization of Grain*. It was organized by the Association of Scientific Centre for the Study of Traditions in the Mediterranean. The main aim of the association is the search of bread-baking traditions in the Mediterranean area, to draw attention to that rich cultural heritage. In Italy, even bread is baked with great creativity and mastery. Different types of bread in the form of a basket with little birds on its handle, a harvested tree with fruits, and even roots were exhibited in a small conference room. The most interesting aspect for me was the presentation made by the famous anthropologist and professor of La Sapienza University, Alberto Mario Cirese. He talked about his deprived childhood during the Second World War and about bread baking in Sardinia, while I was thinking about how much we have in common in our cultures where bread is the very essence of life. Bread baking is an art, and not only in Italy. These cultural aspects indicate how much people have much in common throughout the world.

In this sense of what we all have in common, I always keep in mind one Kazakh legend about the ages of man. God asked a man and animals to come one day to define their way of living. Firstly, He called a man and gave him thirty years to live a happy life without hardships. Then He called a donkey and gave him fifty years to live "Your life won't be easy as you have to carry heavy things, and you will be punished and beaten, and your food won't be tasty." The donkey pleaded for God to give him only thirty years, not fifty since it had to live a hard life. At this moment the man came up and asked for the twenty years that the donkey rejected. The next was a dog. God told him: "Your responsibility is to guard a man's house. You will stay outside and eat bones. You will live to forty!" The dog also pleaded with God to shorten his age by half as its life would be hard, too. Again the man asked for dog's twenty years. The last was a monkey. God said: "You are a stupid creature, and you will entertain people, especially children. You will live for sixty years!" The monkey fell to its knees and asked God to shorten its age by half as it didn't want to live so long being a fool. Again the man came up and asked for monkey's thirty years. So, the man lived his thirty years given by God happily without hardships. From thirty to fifty he lived the donkey's life by passing through hardships, taking responsibilities, creating his family and business. From fifty to seventy the man lived the dog's life guarding what he created. After seventy the man lost his mind, becoming as senseless as a monkey.

According to this fable, mankind was originally meant to live a happy life. God gave us life to enjoy it by raising kids, working, travelling, communicating, learning languages, doing sports, helping each other. We were supposed to live happily but it didn't matter for how long. But we were greedy and self-centered, and in the end this was foolish. There is a book that has been around for quite a while, which tells the lessons of life from a very simple perspective, claiming that all the author ever really need to know he learned in kindergarten. Regardless of the level you take his words on, the message is the same: "...no matter how old you are –when you go out into the world, it is best to hold hands and stick together"[1]. This works on a child's level, and on a cultural level.

In relation to life cycles in different cultures, I was recently honored by being asked to cut fetters, the ceremony called *tusaukeser* (the Kazakh name for cutting fetters), which is held when the baby makes its first steps.

All I Really Need to Know I Learned in Kindergarten. By Robert Fulghum It is an old Kazakh custom which is followed widely nowadays in our country. The legs of the baby are loosely tied with colorful string signifying the diversity of life, which a boy or girl learn to pass through. Then an honored person cuts the string and, by holding the baby by the hands, helps the child make its first steps on a white cloth covered with rose petals. Sweets are thrown on the cloth for the participants to pick up, as it is believed that the feast brings good luck. Kazakhs also believe that after the ceremony a child takes its first steps firmly and without help. This custom is usually accompanied by blessings, songs and wishes for a baby and followed by the feast. In old times after *tusaukeser* a child was presented with a horse and saddle, and nowadays with toys and fancy clothes. According to the custom, the honor to cut fetters is given to a woman who has her own children, who has experience in life and is respected. When the parents of a baby called to invite me to partic-

---

[1] P.6. All I Really Need to Know I Learned in Kindergarten. By Robert Fulghum.

ipate in the ceremony, at that moment I felt deeply honored. It was my first experience to perform that kind of ceremony for a beautiful little girl whose name was Enlik, dressed in a white national dress with a coned hat decorated with feathers, fur and pearls. Two grandmothers from both sides came from Kazakhstan to take part in the ceremony. I wish Enlik all the best with every step she makes in her life! By the way, I saw Enlik two weeks after the ceremony — she was standing firmly on her feet.

This very meaningful tradition made me think over the issues of the cultural fetters of a foreigner in the diversity of the world. Making the first steps in a new culture, we find this process interesting, informative, curious. We make comparisons and our personal judgments. We have to adjust, not only tolerate but to respect the differences among people, absorb the cultures we encounter, to live with openness to all the possibilities this life affords. As one author said about being abroad: "… everyone goes on missing the point, until you finally give up trying to make it and either go back to … or adjust in silence. This is what culture shock really means, either making your own peace, or leaving."[2] There is another tradition I also took part in recently. When a child is born, Kazakhs don't show newly born babies to anybody except their close family members until he or she is forty days old. We believe that a child is too vulnerable and fragile to be exposed to the world the first month or so. When a baby reaches forty days old, only women are invited to perform the

---

[2] P.29. Coming Home Crazy. By Bill Holm.

ceremony. Women put a baby in a tub filled with water, a few coins are placed on the bottom of the tub, and with a silver spoon the most respected woman pours water on a child's head and body, giving blessings at the same time, and then she trims the baby's hair and nails for the first time. The rest of the women also give blessings, and help to perform the ceremony. The infant is dressed and shown to everybody. The women who participate receive gifts and are invited to a party in honor of the baby. In this case, the baby was a boy with light grey eyes, named Asylkhan. A bit later, young parents of another boy, Amir, invited me to take part in this meaningful tradition. What an experience!

I must say that in our culture we adults try to adjust to the needs of a child whether he or she is a newly born or older. Our kids from their first days wear charm bracelets or pins to protect against the evil eye. People avoid admiring a child, as staring at a child is considered to be rude.

In sharp contrast, children abroad seem to be more independent than our kids in Kazakhstan and seem to adjust to adults and their way of living. They crawl barefoot on cold floors in the airports, travelling with their parents from the moment they are born, and they would put all sorts of foreign objects into their mouth and no one tells them not to. They drink soft drinks and eat potato chips from early childhood, and they can sit for hours in their prams while their parents shop. And children attend kindergartens even if sick. I watched a woman holding a four-month-old baby in a bar where she came to smoke and drink a glass of wine, and I watched a baby crawling around a pool while his mother was in the house busy with other things. These apparently loose ties between people may lead to behavior which may be simply thoughtless but appears to be rude when teenagers on a bus, for example, do not give their seats to elderly people.

When our granddaughter had a high fever, I called the Italian doctor we used to see time to time but she refused to visit a patient saying "non é grave" (nothing serious). In our country if a child has a temperature over 38°, no one discusses the issue — a doctor or an ambulance comes. On another occasion, I was quite in despair when having a neck problem. An Italian professor told me to wear a neck corset for a month, while a Russian professor told me not to do that. Living in Italy at that time I took the side of Russian professor and it worked. Different attitudes, different views on one and the same problem. Sometimes it is hard to make a reasonable choice especially in medicine. I chose the side of a Russian professor because I knew him and because our cultures are close in treating people. In general, we trust our doctors and their decisions are final. Abroad, to my mind, it is up to a patient to make a choice. Doctors seem to be reluctant to take responsibility. Recently I had to stop by in Austria to see a doctor because of an unexpected pain. I knew which medicine helped me in that case. The doctor examined me and said that in fact the medicine I was talking about could really help me but he couldn't take responsibility prescribing injections. When I was about to leave without any cure, he handed me an injection I needed and said he hadn't given it to me. It took me another half an hour to get to the place to be injected by my daughter, not the doctor. We had to choose between being operated on or not when we saw an English doctor who said it was parents' decision or, in other words, the parents' responsibility to operate on our daughter for tonsillitis. My husband said we had better go home since we had a choice. He felt sorry for Asem and I insisted on the operation though I also felt sorry for her. Until the last minute I felt under stress. I can encounter many stressful situations regarding medical issues and sometimes I just made my mind to go back to our country to get proper treatment with less stress. Besides, it takes less time to do it because you make arrangements with the people you know.

Collecting cross-cultural observations is what our family is fond of. Every Wednesday, when I attend French and German classes, I pass nice Waterloo areas in Brussels and notice a friendly sign with a picture of a little dog: *Ici, je suis tenu en laisse* (Here, I am tied to a leash) or *C'est moi qui habite ici* (It's me who lives here). In Olgiata, a quiet and green area outside of Rome where we used to walk the kids and admire nature around us, big houses with huge gardens and always big barking dogs had signs on gates, like *Sono di guarda qui* (I am a guard here). These signs sound cautioning but friendly. I remember quite opposite warnings in my country: "Beware, mad dog!" I hope this attitude in Kazakhstan towards dogs has changed by now.

When our children and grandchildren started kindergartens, schools, and universities abroad, we kept telling them that since we were the first Kazakh diplomats in the

USA and in Spain, they were also the first representatives of our country. "Whatever you do, whatever you say, people around you will judge our country by you," we kept reminding them. And they didn't disappoint us.

Our children grew up cross-culturally learning to interact in environments that were different from their own and adjusting to the new ways of life. Our grandchildren are growing up open-minded. We wanted them to be able to appreciate where they came from, to be familiar with their own cultural identity and to learn more about the culture of the host country and respect the differences among people. We are all more alike than unlike, we are all members of the human family. Recognizing this, our grandchildren, I trust, will cut their own cultural fetters and help others cut theirs.

CHAPTER IV
GOOD PEOPLE ARE ALWAYS THERE

"Cherish your human connections: your relationships with friends and family."

Joseph Brodsky

The last conversation class in Italian was almost over. Mariella, our class teacher, put aside the papers and said that soon we would all leave Italy and she would like to know what we thought about the country.It was a group of women from different countries andMarie-Dominique, a pleasant woman from France, was the first to leave Italy. She said that she had many friends from all over the world but she couldn't name any Italian to be among her friends. Mariella did not expect her to say that and started mumbling about the difference between Milanese and Romans (she had lived in Milan for a long time), that probably Romans were not easy to deal with and so on. When she asked me whatmy opinion about it was, I said that Marie Dominique was right.

There were many Italians that we were friendly with, that we admired, but none that we had an intimate friendship with. Not once had we been invited to visit an Italian home, except when we had classes on different subjects, like decoupage, quilting, painting, etc.. Italians prefer to meet foreigners outside of their homes. They tend to go on vacation at the same beach, spend week- ends at certain places with familiar people. They are bound to the same environments and same habits. Like Japanese or Chinese, Italians tend to travel abroad in groups. In our culture, people prefer travelling as couples or families. While abroad, rarely would they look for their countrymen. Usually they would try to speak a foreign language, mainly English, and pretend they don't understand Kazakh or Russian when standing next to you in a shop and hearing your conversation in the mother tongue.

After having lived eight years in Italy, we were invited to a private party for the first time where everybody knew each other except us. Only a few times did we receive an invitation to an Italian wedding ceremony from people we barely knew. It happened because somebody wanted to show his openness (and his elegance) to the foreigners. Another *"bella figura"* (image).

Making friends abroad is a matter of getting close to the culture of your posting, having interest in everyday life of the people around you. You feel isolation at the beginning, and perhaps you feel depressed, especially when you do not speak the language of your posting. And if you let this initial stage go without any attempt to change for good on your part, nobody will do it for you and you will remain alone.

When we came back to Kazakhstan from England, Asem went to American school. There was another Kazakh girl in their grade but she felt herself isolated, as nobody talked to her despite that she spoke English, and she had not been invited into any circles of friends. At first that girl thought she has been isolated because she was the only native in the class of foreigners. When Asem entered the class, the girl became more upset because Asem was accepted immediately by the class. The poor girl did not realize that it was her own mistake. She didn't make an attempt to socialize. She was waiting for a move from the foreign students; she was waiting for acceptance. And she probably defined "acceptance" in her own way.

When our granddaughter Dayana went back to Kazakhstan after seven years (since birth) in Italy, she instinctively chose foreigners in her class to socialize with. We used to live among Italians and kept up the Russian language at home, at kindergarten, and later at the Russian embassy school. We used to go to a local sports club, our kids were invited to Italian birthday parties, making Italian friends as well. Dayana and her cousin Arlan envied their Russian classmates, who would spend time together after school as they lived in a compound, whereas our grandchildren would go home and play by themselves. Occasionally we invited their schoolmates to our house but it was not enough for them. We truly felt sorry for them, but could do lit- tle else for them. We could see that a lack of socializing with the same-age schoolmates coming from the same culture affected our grandchildren as they were growing up. Children learn the skills of interpersonal interaction socializing with the peer group, which exerts a most powerful social influence on the child.

They say: "The world is a book and those who do not travel read only one page."

I must admit that our grandchildren began to read this book at a very early age. In fact, they were international from birth. They were surrounded by people of different nationalities with their nanny and ballet instructor from Ukraine, Italian neighbors, Italian doctors, Italian swimming coach, Russian teachers. The grandchildren distinguish our national flag from others (we've got it at the entrance of our residence and, of course, at the embassy), *Astana* (our capital) is their favorite book as it is colorful and big, *Jingle Bells* is their favorite song to dance, *Lion King* is the favorite animated cartoon to watch. They like to talk about planets and the solar system, volcanoes and dinosaurs, their future plans, things they would like to do on their own when they finally grow up. Perhaps their sense of growing up is broader than if they had not been exposed to international situations.

Thanks to our children and grandchildren, contacts with our neighbors, ex-pats and local people are often more easily made. In Spain, when Asem attended American school, we made friends with some parents of Asem's classmates. We used to drive our kids to school and pick them up after school, have coffee while waiting for them in a neighboring cafeteria, invite and be invited to children's birthday parties. We still keep in touch with Yorie Sakamaki from Japan, Anne Wilde from the USA through the American school in Madrid, Anne Ostby from Norway through the American school in Kazakhstan. Nowadays Facebook helps us to keep in touch and updated on each other's lives.

Twelve years ago in Madrid I met my best friend, Irene Koch, an American now living in Alicante, Spain. At that time we were posted in Madrid, Spain, and our residence was in Boadilla del Monte, a somewhat rural- feeling area just outside of Madrid (a location chosen because of the closeness to the American school of Madrid where Asem studied). Across the street from our house lived Irene and her husband Thomas and their two little boys, Jonas and Lucas. We often recall how we met each other. It was Halloween evening. Irene, dressed in a witch costume, was passing along our street with her Lucas (in a wheelchair due to a disabling disease) and Jonas with his friends in different Halloween costumes. They stopped by our house and I went out to give sweets to the kids. We talked a bit and the next day we were invited for coffee in Irene's house. Ever since then I don't remember a day without her! We had so much fun going out, talking, watching videos (our favorite is *Thelma and Louisa*), dancing Sevillanas, decorating eggs, taking part in charity events, and on and on.

Irene is charged with positive energy! She always smiles and she is honest, open, and generous. She is a true friend and confidante. I consider myself to be blessed to have a friend like Irene. I also have lots of energy, but Irene has twice my energy and understands me better than anybody else. She often keeps saying that she is more

Kazakh than American. I would say I am more international than Kazakh.

Another amazing person I met in Spain was Nur, a princess from Jordan, who at the time of our meeting was a wife of ambassador of Jordan to Spain. Though a princess, she never poses, but rather is natural, sincere, and a faithful friend. She also has three multi-cultural children. She knows a lot, she is a good listener, she has a rich experience in life. She is a person who brings peace into your heart; she never rushes, and I learned from her to be patient with others. It is rare to find and make friends with people with different cultural and educational backgrounds. But when you meet them, you understand how close they become to you, you need them and you deeply miss them when they are far from you.

In Italy I met three ladies much older than myself with whom I developed deep bonds: Ratna Effendi, Maria Manfredi, and Mariella Sansalvadore. Ratna was the president of International Women's Club when I met her. Energetic, responsible, hardworking person, of Indonesian origin, made the club function, the club which comprised about 200 women, each of different status and background. To organize groups of people is always difficult, to find common interests, and to unite women coming from different countries is not easy. Her priority was dealing with people, to inspire people to work to a common goal.

Maria Manfredi was my tutor, I would say. Creative, talented, well-mannered, patient. Hobbies and crafts united us much more than anything else. She would call me to say she found something interesting to work with and I would come to share our common passion towards crafts. Her talent is to be helpful and innovative.

Mariella Sansalvadore is a person who enriches others spiritually. For decades she has been working in the European Union to represent Italy. Two years ago she was given an award from the Italian government and I am proud for her. As a member of the club, she led the conversational class for foreigners. Thanks to these conversations, which were cultural exchanges, we learned a lot about each other.

People we meet leave imprints on our lives, as some become dear friends and change our life, some remain friends we keep in touch with, some want to be sure we are in good shape and in a good mood, and some want to keep a good memory of us. "When we honestly ask ourselves which person in our lives means the most to us, we often find that it is those who, instead of giving advice, solutions, or cures, have chosen rather to share our pain and touch our wounds with a warm and tender hand. The friend who can be silent with us in a moment of despair or confusion, who can stay with us in an hour of grief and bereavement, who can tolerate not knowing, not curing, not healing and face with us the reality of our powerlessness, that is a friend who cares," said Henri J.M. Nouwen, a Dutch writer. And this describes my friends.

Both Almaz and I come from big families. He has three sisters and two brothers and I have four younger sisters. He is the eldest among brothers with two elder sisters. Being the eldest reflects our life even abroad because you always keep in mind your responsibility towards the younger ones even if they are in their forties and fifties. Like many first-born children, I learned to care for my sisters. My sisters keep reminding me that I am not only the eldest sister in our family but I also replaced our late father and beloved late grandmother. This is the way we are raised in our country –to feel part of the family wherever you are.

My mother-in-law passed away when we were in Great Britain. She had a stroke and had been in bed for six years. The family of Almaz, very united and obedient towards their parents, went through deep grieving together without accepting any outside help. We offered to pay for the hospital care for them but they rejected the offer, saying that it was the duty of children to care for their mother. My husband had been feeling guilty constantly throughout his mother's illness, and his authoritarian father often reminded him of his duties towards the family and especially to his parents (though the reminding was not necessary). Almaz is a very sensitive person. His youngest brother still lives with their father, who turned ninety this year. Every time Almaz visits his father he feels depressed because of not being able to take care for his father and because of living so far away from him. He never argues with his father, whatever his father might say; he keeps calling his father every Friday, and has for the last forty years after having left his family to study at the university in another city. He buys medicine for his father, he hides his smoking from his father, though his father knows Almaz smokes a lot. He supports his father financially, arranges his father's birthday parties, and attends those parties almost every year; and he arranged his father's trip to Spain when we were posted there.

I have not seen my father-in-law for a long time, and neither have our children. We made a visit to get his father's blessings before our first trip to the US. Five years later, before going to Great Britain, we visited them again. We spent two weeks with them, the two last weeks, when my mother-in-law could still sit at the table, weak, pale as a shadow and tired of the disease. Almaz and I returned to Kazakhstan when she died. Asem, who was eleven at that time, cried to hear about her grandmother. Only after my mother-in-law's death did I realize I did not know her very well, that I would have learned a lot from her. She was a strong woman, intelligent, forth- right. She never forgot anything. I wished to talk to her sometimes as I found her to be a good listener but she was not talkative at all. She could spend the whole day without saying a word to anybody. Almaz inherited her ability to keep silent.

I remember one episode which happened when we visited them right after our marriage. My husband's youngest sister was cleaning the house and at one point her brother threw his shirt away, being disorderly and they both started quarrelling. Their mother came in and, without saying a word and without finding out who was right and who was wrong, she gently sent her son away and left. I had never seen a speechless scene like that before. The kids always felt the power of their mother even if she did not talk to them very much. I would make a scene instead but I learned that conflicts can be resolved silently. Silence can be loud. Once I did the same with our twins when they were fighting. I tapped both of them on the back without saying a word. Our twins remembered that incident because it was a unique speechless scene.

Unfortunately, I don't have close ties with my mother. Whatever I was doing, I received no encouragement ever from my mother. There is still a big gap of misunderstanding between us, and not only between her and me but also between my sisters and her. She lives with one of my sisters, and we all deeply care about her, of course, but there is no mother's response and under- standing. I am a grandmother myself but I still need a motherly shoulder to lean on sometimes.

I was very close to my grandmother, though, who died twenty years ago. She was a powerful figure in my life. Kind, creative, wise, sincere, and loving. She spoke only Kazakh, so I always wondered how she managed to talk to Russian neighbors, who loved her. She would go shopping and if she forgets money to take with her the shop owner would ask her not to worry about the money and bring it next time. She was extremely honest and therefore was trusted. Not knowing the alphabet, she couldn't read, and I taught her how to put her signature on papers.

Her life was tough. She was actually my late father's aunt, so she was in fact my great-aunt, but I thought of her as my grandmother. When my grandfather was exiled and later shot for his political beliefs, and his wife died the same year from being sick, my father, who was seven years old, and his youngest brother of five were left alone. Their aunt took in both boys and raised them as her kids.

Her husband died in Smolensk, a Russian city, during the Second World War. They didn't have their own kids. She kept a paper all her life about her husband's death after one of the military attacks at the very beginning of the war. It was a torn, yellow piece of paper that she used to wrap in a white cloth. We used to go to the soldiers' grave in one of our central parks of Almaty every May ninth, the Victory Day over the Nazis. Almaz and I promised her that we would find his grave one day. We hope to fulfill that promise.

She was a hard-working woman, and I still remember her hands, wrinkled, dry but so warm and flexible. She would wake up at five in the morning and prepare breakfast for the whole family, then wake us up at different times according to our timetable, do our hair, as four of us had braids, clean the house, and do shopping. By ten in the morning everything was ready! She even attended PTA meetings held in Russian. My sisters and I used to recite poems about grandmas at school performances at Women's Day and, before going to bed, we would pray for her. I thought my grandma gave birth to me and I even insisted on that and my girl friends would laugh at me. We learned a lot from her. Now I know I have her sense of being creative. I only wish that I could talk to her, get her opinion, and wonder what she would have thought about this or that. She is my guardian angel. I used to see her in my dreams at night, and in this way I thought I was protected by her. I see her now less and less in my dreams but I still hope she protects us all.

I also lost my best friend in Kazakhstan two years ago. It was hard for me to realize that Nadejda (Russian name for "hope") was gone. I heard the news about her in Italy, and I couldn't help crying for several days. She visited us two years ago in Rome and we had time to recall our youth together. Lately I found her postcards to me with her own verses which I had kept for many years. Nadejda had an excellent memory and was deeply devoted to her friends. She would never forget a birthday and would come any time she was needed. All our mutual friends in Kazakhstan were moved by my ongoing grief. I explained to them that the distance made my grief worse; I didn't have anybody to support me except my immediate family. I still miss my friend.

As the time passes, being away from your home base, your country, makes you think over family relationships in a more acute, sensitive way. Our parents are old and weak, while our sisters and brothers have their own problems and sometimes don't even share them with us as we are so far away and occupied with our own daily situations, especially the diplomatic job we have been sent to do.

Every time we speak to my husband's father, and this is becoming progressively more rare, as he gets older and older and has hearing problems, he reminds us to tell our kids where they come from, who their grandmother and grandfather are; he wants us to remind them to learn and speak Kazakh, not to lose their roots. After my mother-in-law's death, I and our kids almost lost contact with them, except with my husband's youngest brother. We often talk to him and share our concerns. There is an eleven-year difference between us. But, as often happens, we do not choose people, fate does. When I first entered their family at the age of twenty-two, his youngest brother was eleven, he was less busy than other family members were, and he supported me in many ways, as I was shy and did not feel comfortable at the beginning. He would take me out, give me chocolates which their mother would hide from them, talk to me, and ask me to cook something unusual, and he would help me in the kitchen. We still have this kind of relationship of openness, and sincerity. He has twin daughters like we have, which also helped to build a bridge of understanding and trust between us.

When we go home, nobody is interested in our life abroad. People usually have no idea how busy I am abroad as the wife of an ambassador. We wives of ambassadors don't get much sympathy and find understanding only in the same circle. That's why I hardly tell anyone about what they assume to be my "stylish" life. The usual question I am asked by my countrymen sounds like this with some variations: "What do you possibly do abroad?" As if I just sleep all day long, don't cook as I have a cook, don't drive myself as I have a driver.

I guess we have a bad and lazy image.

Before leaving for abroad, I didn't know, either, what my duties and responsibilities would be. A lot is written about diplomacy, and very little and close to nothing about wives of diplomats, such as ambassadors, how they adapt, what they are busy with, what kind of activities they are involved with, etc.. Once, in Italy, my husband called me an "image-maker of the embassy", as I used to make presentations about Kazakhstan, invite people for lunch and dinner, and was actively involved in charity. It is true, we are image-makers of our countries. Foreigners judge us by our appearance, by our behavior. I often hear foreigners ask: "Are all Kazakhs like you?" At one of the charity bazaars in Spain, one Spanish gentleman came up to our table. He noticed the name of our country and was silent for a moment recalling where he could possibly have heard about Kazakhstan. Then he exclaimed: "Gulistan!" My best friend Irene keeps saying: "Gulistan from Kazakhstan". I am glad my name is directly associated with my country.

Living abroad, we develop a wide range of relationships, a rich international network. I used to think that the younger we are, the easier new relationships are established. Of all three children we have, the youngest Asem has as many friends, as one might imagine from the vast geography of her encounters. She can travel to almost any country in the world and find a friend. Asem has a talent for attracting people, making friends, and keeping in touch with them. She remembers her friends' birth dates and significant moments of their lives, and she is very sensitive to their problems and concerns. She is helpful as a true friend should be. I am also lucky to meet people and make friends with people having different cultural backgrounds. I have now more foreign friends than friends from my own country. Now, I know for sure: friendship is established at any age and in any place. The more we travel, the more friends we are apt to have. Every Christmas time, when I send letters to my friends, I add new names in my address book which starts from the US. Yes, some names disappear from those pages, because of those who pass away, but, new names appear in this endless cycle of life.

We develop relationships with friends on a deeper level because friends from different countries constitute a part of our lives abroad — sometimes, a significant part. We all leave a part of our hearts behind with friends and families when leaving a country, and relationships are valued because they give us a sense being connected with countries we have lived in. And as my best friend defines our friendship in the following way: *"No es coincidencia, sino diosidencia* (It's not coincidence, it's God-cidence)". Real friendship is truly divine. And tried and true friends, like close family, do not appear by accident in your life: good people are always there, whether in your heart or by your side.

CHAPTER V

ON EXPERIENCES AND CHALLENGES

*"Don't limit your challenges.
Challenge your limits."*

Anonymous

In a past life I could have been born English as I love the English language and I love challenges. Especially challenges. In the USA, when my husband told me once that it would be hard for me to learn to drive a car, I took the challenge. I called a driver's training school, spent only ten hours learning to drive, passed the test and got the driver's license, which I needed in the US mainly as a document. A driver's license in the States is more important than an identity document. But I did not have my own car, so I drove my husband's car occasionally in the US. In England, however, my American driver's license had been changed to the English one, and then into Spanish one when we moved to Spain. In Italy, I could use a Kazakhstan driver's license. In Spain we had a driver and there was no need for me to drive a car. But I preferred driving sometimes and actually learned the hard way there, with several minor bumper jumpers (with no consequences, thankfully!)

Our daughters got their driver's licenses abroad, in England and Italy. It was not even a challenge for them — it was a necessity. "Learning to drive for the first time and doing it in UK was a big mistake," said Asel once. She meant that they drove on the left side in the United Kingdom as opposed to the right as is the case in Kazakhstan or most other parts of the world.

I saw a computer for the first time when I was thirty-eight! The computer was meant for the whole family and everybody had an access to it except me. I wasn't caught up in studies, nor had a particular job, so there was no need for me to use the computer at that time. But then I took the challenge again. I signed up for the computer course in Washington, D.C.. The class was for free, the group was big, and I learned only the basics.

This challenge is still tough for me, though I know how to use e-mail, open browser to go online, search with Google, use Skype with my friends and family, buy tickets online, attach files to e-mails and open attachments, print, edit a text, scan documents, and use USB and flash cards. I still type with two fingers though, which I know is a bad habit. I would not know the difference between an iPhone and an iPod. I don't know how to draw charts. For me technology must be simple to use. I have always relied on my family to help out with my high-tech gadgets, whether my phone or my tablet or my computer. I have no cyber secrets from my family, since everybody needs to know my password to help me with this or that operation. When my children visit me, they play with the choice of the ring tone on my phone and download books and music on my tablet. They go on about smart technology and new user-friendly gadgets and make sure I have the latest.

I have lady friends who send me messages through their children. I am happy to be able to send messages myself. I prefer email Internet to phone calls, actual Christmas cards and letters sent in envelopes to Internet wishes. I do not use a camera in my iPhone, as I use a small digital camera and prefer printing photos rather than having them in cell phones.

My big challenge in Italy was painting. I tried watercolor, switched to acrylic colors, and I am dreaming of oil painting. I am grateful to my painting teachers, Gabriella Delmastro and later Erica Angioletti, two great Italian painters. I was "blind" before I started painting. I looked at skies and saw only one color: blue. Now I notice more things around me, admire whole ranges of colors and try to see what other people in a hurry might not see. Because of my Italian teachers, I know the Italian words for brushes, colors, and canvas. I managed to exhibit my works in Italy twice among other professional and amateur painters.

My first hobby was egg painting with wax. I learned this craft from Fusia, the wife of the ambassador of Malaysia accredited to Spain, who learned it from wife of ambassador of Sweden, though it is a Ukrainian tradition. Fusia showed the technique of egg painting to us, a group of wives of diplomats, only two times and it turned out to be difficult and time-consuming. First, you have to select chicken, goose or duck eggs, find smooth ones without cracks, and then you have to wash them, wipe them dry, and make a design using a pencil. With a special pointed tool you put wax on the surface of an egg following the design. Then you dip the egg into natural batik colors, wipe it and apply another wax design and repeat the process the number of times you feel is appropriate. Practice makes perfect. It is one of the those meditative crafts that both focuses your attention and vacates all other thoughts. Like painting, it deepens your sensitivity to shapes and colors and the infinite variety of beauty in the world.

When we moved to Italy, we had been waiting a month for the credentials to be granted and we were not able to participate officially in any event or activity.

If it were not for the egg painting, my spare time might have been filled with restlessness rather than creativity. I did my best creations at that time. After a while, in fact, I gave my first class in egg painting to other wives of diplomats accredited to Italy. This added a dimension of socializing, in the sense of learning from each other and sharing knowledge with others by experimenting, practicing and using imagination. By encouraging each other, we believe that together we can do anything. Creativity unites people. The study concludes that excellence is determined by opportunities, encouragement, training, motivation and most of all, practice. No one reached high levels of achievement in their field without devoting thousands of hours of serious training.

I like detailed work, to see or do. Working in detail comforts me though I am impatient. I can sit knitting, making jewelry, sewing for hours. I learned egg painting with wax, and I would like to decorate plates, either wooden or porcelain. I envision myself sitting for hours decorating them. I see myself in a workshop, in the room with other painters. Everybody is concentrated, silent, white robes, big windows, jars and plates around. Experimenting, discovering. A dream.

Challenges make you discover things about yourself that you never really knew. For example, in Spain I became unexpectedly interested in dancing Sevillanas, a complex popular folk dance from southern Spain (originally the Seville area, as the name implies). I joined a group of wives of ambassadors and diplomats from different countries to start the class. Thanks to Sevillanas I met new people and made friends with some of them. It was Marisa Torres Belinchón who did her best to teach us. She is a wonderful person and my dear friend. It took me three years to learn this four-part dance. The first year I trained my feet and the second year my arms; the third year I learned to coordinate my arms and feet. And suddenly I was dancing (more or less). Every time I visit my friends in Spain, I take this opportunity to practice the dance. What a privilege!

In Madrid, as well as other cities, there are places where people come to dance only Sevillanas. Women and men, young and old have one passion: a dance which also unites people. There are so many variations of this dance and every Spaniard improvises on the spot. Probably, you have to be born a Spaniard to be able to understand the soul of the dance. Many Spanish children learn this dance as soon as they take their first steps. We foreigners don't have this advantage, and the Spanish are quite indulgent with our efforts. In fact, we had the rare opportunity to dance it in front of Queen Sofia of Spain during a charity event organized by the diplomatic association in Madrid. After the performance the Queen approached us and asked me (I guess she chose me because I was the only Asian in the group) whether I found Sevillanas to be difficult to learn. I said it was difficult, indeed, for me but it was a good practice and a chance to learn more about Spanish culture. She said that she had tried but she was not able to perform the dance. Maybe for her Greek origin.

Every April, lovers of Sevillanas go to Seville, the capital of Andalusia, to take part in a big festival, the Spring Fair. People from all over Spain, and all over the world, travel to Seville. Some go by train, raucous people dressed in colorful flamenco dresses and suits. The women have frilled dresses often with the traditional polka dots, wear big combs in their hair, and adorn themselves with lavish jewelry (a lot is traditional bijouterie). The men often wear striped grey trousers, white ruffled shirts, black jackets and flat-topped straight-brimmed hats. I attended the Spring Fair twice to watch and take part in this spectacular event. There are more than thousand *casetas* (tents) at the Fair where there are ongoing Sevillanas performances, and most of the tents are privately owned. People invite families and friends to their *casetas*, and celebrate together with unending food and drinks, and they sing and dance with each other, in a family setting.

Whatever we do, wherever we go, whoever we meet and whatever problem we deal with, we get experience. I find myself now insatiable for this sort of experience. I don't even know whether I need this or that kind of experience, I just want the experience. Abroad I have more opportunities to learn because I socialize more, and I have more interactions with other cultures. I can make a flower arrangement, I can organize a party, a reception for fifty, five-hundred people, a charity bazaar, etc.. It is all part of gathering experiences.

With all this experience, for our whole life, we go through one crisis after another. We have crises as little children, as adolescents, as young adults, as newlyweds, as new parents, as parents of older children, and the crises keep coming at us. While age might bring wisdom, it can also bring along a set of complicated issues that can seem overwhelming, which can lead to mid-life stress. When I was confronted with my mid- life crisis, I was totally unprepared, especially for the menopause stage in my life when we were in Spain. I thought it would happen much later or I would not feel it at all, and I didn't realize at first what was happening to me. I heard that Asian women didn't suffer so much, as they used a lot of soy (which contains estrogen) but I didn't use soy at all, except when eating Japanese food. I struggled alone with mood swings, hot flashes, insomnia. It was unnerving at times. It was one of the hardest challenges yet. I was not ready for this challenge. It was not a computer course or a new language to take or leave. Any event can become a crisis if it wipes out our ability to make sense out of what is happening. We feel helpless. It is only after we regain some sense of understanding and some sense of control that we begin to meet the challenge. They say, without challenges there is no progress. What if you cannot meet a challenge?

I was set back at the beginning. Had I been back home, I would have talked to my female friends, or sisters, or I would have seen a doctor. But in a foreign country I didn't feel comfortable talking about my symptoms. Though later, as it lasted a long time, when I had hot flashes during receptions, and some women would ask me if I was O.K. (I was obviously not O.K.), I would say frankly that menopause would kill me, and we would laugh and talk a bit about it. Once, when it happened to me at one of the Asian receptions, and I was as forthright as always, an Asian lady advised me not to talk about it, as it was personal. To her it sounded taboo.

There are many cultural taboos, and some can be harmful. My point of view on this subject is that menopause is a physical change in a woman's body, and every middle-aged woman passes through this stage. If we keep silent, we may perpetuate prejudices and misunderstandings, but if we speak out, we can help each other, and society as a whole, to understand this very natural condition and how to cope with it. Menopause should be discussed not only with doctors, women, and lady friends but also with husbands, mothers, and daughters. My mother never mentioned her experience to me, as if it had never happened to her. Later, when I found out I was going through menopause, I did not have the benefit of her wisdom. Rather, I got all possible information through Internet and I discussed it with my husband, who was also unaware of what was happening to me all of a sudden. We both felt a relief. I like one of doctor's recommendations to the couples: "It's a chance to learn a few new steps in the relationship dance, and set a tone of caring that can last for years". This is even harder than Sevillanas, and even more rewarding.

Our daughters have their own experiences on adapting to new environments, learning languages, on raising their kids, on taking challenges. I asked them to write about their personal experiences and challenges that had led them to a sort of revelation.

Asem, for instance, learned quite a lot about Swiss culture by learning Swiss German, dealing with daily situations. She and her husband, Marcus, opened their own business in Zurich. And this is what Asem says:

I moved to Zurich in January 2010. I did not know anyone, had no job, and did not speak any German. The first thing I did was sign up for a German course. Through that course I got to know a lot of wonderful women, most of them in the same situation as me: they had moved to Zurich because of their husbands and were now trying to learn German and find a job. Three years later we still meet twice a month for coffee to practice our German and catch up on news.

Learning German in Switzerland is not an easy task. One learns High German in the classroom but hears Swiss German on the street and in everyday life. When you are a beginner learning High German, Swiss German sounds like a completely different language. Although officially there is no such thing as written Swiss German and it is considered a dialect of German, if you ask most Swiss Germans they will tell you that High German is for them a «Fremdsprache», a foreign language, and understandably so. They learn Swiss German at home a long time before they learn High German at school, they speak it on the street, at work, and a lot of the young people even text in Swiss German (I receive texts only in Swiss German from the girl working for me at the restaurant). Once you get a good command of High German, you start to understand Swiss German little by little but only when people speak slowly and clearly. Once I mastered High German, I could understand Swiss German from Zurich. The next challenge, which I am currently faced with, is understanding the other dialects of the German part of Switzerland: Bernese German, Wallis German, Basler German, which all sound like different languages in their own right.

When it comes to integration into a society, there is no greater source of information than Internet. It was through meetup.com that I found an Entrepreneurship Meetup that would meet every Tuesday morning at a Starbucks in the middle of town. I knew I wanted to become an entrepreneur, so I wanted to surround myself with like-minded individuals, hear their challenges, share ideas. I met very interesting people with exciting new ventures, businesses, and ideas through this network and I still go to the meetings once a month. It was through a woman I met at one of these meetups that I then found out about the Professional Women's Group of Zurich. The PWG is a group of over 200 women that together create an international career network. We meet once a month to hear inspirational speeches covering a wide range of professional topics and to network together.

This group really inspired me to go further with my entrepreneurship plans. Through it I met very inspiring, very successful women who either owned their own businesses or had very successful careers in large multinationals. When you are embarking on any venture, it is important to surround yourself with positive, successful, like- minded individuals. It was through this network that I learned that you could split virtually any society into YES people and NO people. The Yes people are those who look at a situation and see an opportunity and say YES, let's give it a try. The No people see only the problems and the challenges, they look at a situation and see only the negatives, the reasons NOT to do something, the pitfalls. Those are the people who do not and will never take any risks, and if you don't take any risks, you will never know if something works or not. It was from the women that I met through this network that I knew that I wanted to be a YES person. I had always known that I wanted to be self-employed and own my own business but it was this group and, of course, with the great support of my husband that I finally took on the challenge and the risk of opening up my own restaurant. Being married to a YES person is also a huge advantage. I probably would have never gone through with this huge task if my husband did not support and push me along the way; he gave me and continues to give me a lot of strength in the most difficult moments of this beautiful journey.

There were many reasons why I wanted to open a restaurant in Zurich. First, I wanted to be self-employed. Second, I love food and I love cooking. Third, after spending some time in Zurich, I realized that the city lacked the versatility of London or New York or Barcelona when it came to the food scene. Zurich is a beautiful city, which has a lot to offer, but it still has a long way to go in the development of interesting food concepts, which use fresh, seasonal ingredients. Having lived in countries which such rich culinary backgrounds (Italy, Spain, Kazakhstan), I was missing the same passion in Zurich. I realized, first and foremost, that Zurich lacked a healthy fast-food concept. After a lot of market research, focus groups and writing an entire business plan, I came up with the concept of Simply Soup, a restaurant/takeaway which served fresh, seasonal, homemade soups, salads, and sandwiches. Once the business plan was written, I had to put it into action.

Opening a restaurant in Zurich had some expected, and a lot of unexpected, challenges. We started by doing market research and making a business plan. This was the easy part. Two of the biggest challenges came next: finding an investor and finding the right location. Getting a loan from a bank was out of the question in Switzerland in 2011, as banks all over the world were cutting costs and investing only in proven concepts. We had to revert to the 3Fs of investing: friends, family, and fools.

The second challenge was the biggest of them all. Space in Zurich is limited, whether you are looking for an apartment or a retail space, due to high demand and not enough supply. We searched for a year. We were even willing to go to the outskirts of Zurich. After a whole year, we finally had our big break, a location opened up in the centre of Zurich, just over the bridge from the new stock exchange, around the corner from the headquarters of biggest newspa-

per in Switzerland, and across the street from a large Bank. Our main target market was professional men and women wanting something healthy and fast for lunch, so we knew we struck gold when this location opened up! After some negotiations, both our predecessor (an Italian gentleman having a pasta/wine bar in that location) and the owner of the building agreed to Simply Soup moving in! We took the shop over just before Christmas 2011. We worked for two weeks, straight through the holidays to be able to open on my birthday, January 13th. We completely repainted and redecorated the space, put in new furniture. The last couple of days before the soft opening were the most nerve racking. Due to the holidays everything was coming in last minute: bowls, takeaway packaging, the CHAIRS! We ended up buying provisional chairs from IKEA to be able to open on the 13th. The actual chairs came in two weeks later.

The day of the soft opening was one of the hardest and most nerve-racking experiences I have ever had. I was doing everything for the first time and I had two hundred people coming into the shop that day to judge it! I still cringe when I think about that day or even about the first weeks of opening the restaurant. I am glad I won't have to do it again for the first time. It has now been a whole year since we first opened and I could not be happier. Of course, we still have a lot ahead of us, but so far the ride has been unforgettable. After one year I am proud to say that we have hundreds of happy regular customers, over 250 soup recipes and a concept that is booming. Our next step is to go mobile: Simply Soup will have a food truck which will sell soup all over the city of Zurich. In the not too distant future we are going to open other outlets in Zurich and Switzerland. The goal is to bring healthy and nutritious fast food to as many people as we can.

This journey has been full of ups and downs but I will never regret having taken it and am looking forward to what is coming ahead.

On January 14th, 2013 we had the one year anniversary of Simply Soup. In light of the anniversary, I wanted to do something special. I had recently seen a wonderful speech from Candy Chang, who started the "Before I die I want to..." initiative in the US, which is basically a wall where people can write what they would like to do or accomplish before they die. The idea is to use public space to communicate with people around you about what is important to you and what you really want to do before you die. The idea is not to lose sight of what is really important to us as individuals. I liked this idea very much because for me Simply Soup is something I wanted to do before I die. For me it is a dream come true, it is something I made with my own two hands, and it is important to me. I wanted to create something of my own that can live on when I am long gone. I wanted to create something that adds value to the society we live in. Switzerland is a society where personal privacy is very respected, meaning most of the time you don't know anything about your neighbors, colleagues or just the people you see on a daily basis. I thought the "Before I Die..." initiative could help spark some sharing in this society where everyone goes out of their way to mind their own business. It is interesting to know what people want to do before they leave the earth. So, we made a similar wall in the window of Simply Soup and, so far, my favorites include:

"Before I die I want to... fall completely in love with the universe, live to see aliens, write a book, find my love, feel real love, speak Swiss German, live long, have many babies, find peace, be O.K. with it all".

Asel, our daughter who lives in Astana, Kazakhstan, works for KAZATOMPROM, a big national company. She speaks about challenges taken abroad and back in our country:

I always wanted to work for a big company and bring about change in the organization. I thought about it when I was still doing my BA back in London in 1996. This was the reason I chose International Business as my major instead of studying towards Criminal Psychology degree, which also caught my attention. I remember that I discussed my choice of studies with my parents and they said that "at some point, maybe, you would want to return to Kazakhstan and it would be much easier to find work if you do Business degree". I agreed. Now looking back over the years and 17 years since that decision, I believe that I succeeded in making my wishes come true. I have joined one of the biggest national companies in Kazakhstan back in 2000, and ever since then I stayed loyal to the nuclear industry that the company was part of.

Within these 12 years I have discovered many things about myself. It amazed me how naïve I was about easily making friends and about getting rewards when it comes to initiatives while working for a national Kazakhstan company. The biggest challenge, however, was being able to understand what is required of you. You are not always given specific instructions, there was no protocol to follow, and there were only deadlines and your strict boss, who expected you to come to work early and leave work late in the evening. I remember my first days at work and joining the Sales group with five employees. They were not easy to approach, as they knew (somehow) that I was the daughter of the ambassador and I just came back to Kazakhstan, recently having graduated abroad, and they kept their distance. Everyone was surprised I was given the lowest position within the department to start from, as "people with connections" always take higher positions when they join the first time. So, for my colleagues, I was an "enigma". They often asked: "why did Asel come back to Kazakhstan when she had a choice of staying abroad and why on earth would she choose this company?" Many times I explained how much I missed Kazakhstan and everything about it, that I grew up in this town and I left when I was fifteen, but always wanted to come back and contribute to my society. I always had the same "questioning" look in return and, after many attempts to explain, I gave up. I understand one important thing, that I should stop caring what my colleagues think. This is one of the main differences, that I noticed coming back to my country. People tend to care what others think about them, they care what others say about them, and they try their utmost to change that. I did not want to be affected by this. Abroad I felt more liberated in what I did, what I wore, and what I said.

As I mentioned already, making friends was not easy. I could not openly discuss things with colleagues I was trying to befriend. They would look at how I dressed when we talked, they would ask too many questions about me, but they would not share their own stories so readily. I did not want to be the talker all the time, as listening for me has been a natural habit, but here was the situation when I had to tell stories most of the time and I felt myself to be an entertainer rather than enjoying the company of others. This was also the time when I stumbled across this work-life balance concept. Most of my colleagues would stay at work till very late and come to work early in the morning, and then pride themselves on being very disciplined and complain that they did most of the work in the department.

I felt pressured that I had to do the same, so as not to stick out and bring attention to myself. I was still affected by the what-people-think-about- me virus. But working till late did not contribute to my work. I felt there was still the same amount of it, whether I stayed late or not. It also made me irritable and I had no quality time enjoying life outside work. So, one day I approached my boss and told him that I couldn't stay after 6pm, that I was an early-bird type of person and I just didn't function in the evening well. We agreed that I would come earlier in the morning, so that I could get my work done within regular working hours. My colleagues were surprised that I even questioned the norm and asked for flexibility, as they were very much accustomed to adjust to whatever was given.

When I was later promoted to be the head of four employee units within the Marketing and Sales Department,

I tried to apply same basic principles to my team. During our regular project meetings, I made it clear that my team was welcome to show initiative both group and individual; I asked for timely support and feedback and I asked them to work as a team and not as individuals. I asked every employee in my unit to write individual and group SWOT analysis (strengths, weaknesses, opportunities, and threats), so that I could do my job better by understanding how my team operated, and by learning more about people I worked with. I assigned specific times during the day when employees could approach me with their questions and we could work on things they needed help with.

My husband Khalil happened to be working at the same company but in the different department. And he was worried about me, saying that he would want me to delegate all that stress and use punishment rather than reward policy when it comes to employee motivation. He stressed that if I were to change something, it would have to be done at the senior-executives level, using a top- down approach and even that might not help, as it is necessary to change people's mentality first.

Many times at work, I noticed that "thank yous" were not common. I was very much used to saying "thank you" for almost anything when interacting in the work place (or outside work), but I wouldn't hear people thanking each other very often or saying "please" when asking for something to be done. It is one of those cultural differences one would refer to when you see signs like "don't touch", or "don't lean against the window", or "don't throw objects into..." in the supermarkets, museums, restaurants, etc., the word "please" often being omitted. Words "excuse me" at the beginning of the conversation in a situation when you want to catch someone's attention are also not usual, since people would mostly just say what they want from you and often without any greetings. This you encounter mostly in situations when someone approaches you on the street to ask directions or ask you, for example, if you are the last in the queue.

Men at work always shake hands when greeting each other. The building where we work has thirty- seven floors with around eight hundred employees and only two elevators. In the morning, if you are "lucky", you can get stuck in the elevator with around twelve people stopping at different floors with men shaking each other's hands, sometimes making a big effort to return a hand shake. It's a part of local etiquette.

I am facing a far tougher challenge now that our daughter, Dayana, is living with us in Kazakhstan. Ever since she came back to Kazakhstan in August 2012, after seven wonderful years spent in Rome with my parents, who greatly miss her now, she has been asking questions about why we live where we live. She questions what people talk about, what we do at work, and what language they speak on the street, in school, in the shops. I remember that one time we were not able to drive directly to our apartment building because of a road block (construction works in progress) and this was all done without a prior notice. Dayana commented: "We should sit down all together and write a letter to our President. He can call them and ask to let us into our building". Then she also commented that, maybe, they could let us through because we had a diplomatic license plate! We laughed that day and discussed her observations during dinner. We also explained that in our own country we didn't need diplomatic license plates, because we were country nationals.

My husband, Khalil, and I were glad we chose the right school for Dayana. It is an international school, with children coming from all over the globe, so that she would feel it is not all that different from Italy, where she was used to being surrounded by foreigners and hearing different languages. One of her best friends is a girl from India and we made many attempts to befriend her parents, so that Dayana could spend some time with the girl also outside school. It was always a pleasure, and still was, to catch a word or two with the girl's mother, when we waited in the hallway for our kids to come out. But after my several attempts to get them join us after school for sweets or meet us on the weekend, but them shying away with kind excuses, I gave up trying. I realized that, for some foreigners in Kazakhstan, there was an issue of not easily deciding to make friends as they knew that their time in Kazakhstan was limited to a certain period of time. Perhaps, they didn't want their kids to miss friends too much after leaving, and they chose to keep a distance. Language could also be a barrier for them in this regard, as English was not widely spoken in the city.

Speaking of speaking languages, my favorite is still German even though I feel I am losing it with the years, having less opportunities to practice it (except, of course, when visiting my sister, Asem, and my brother-in-law, Markus, in Zurich or going on business trips to Vienna, where our industry's main international agency is located). German was the first foreign language I learned while in school back in the USSR, when I was eight years old. Three years into studies and I took part in the city Olympics with school competition for knowledge of the German language. I took first place. My motivation to win was my love for the language and my teacher's greatest support. Later, when I had to start speaking German in high school, it was not all that different from learning German, except that we were living in an English-speaking environment. Spanish came next and it felt much easier to learn it, as it was in Spain, where I started attending Spanish courses with my mom. Spaniards cherish their language and they believe the world should speak it too. I had the most fantastic time in Spain while doing my MBA!

I am not particularly a risk taker. I hope I can learn to take risks. We are faced with choices every single day: what to shop for, what books to read, how to find a good doctor. I hope to be more confident in choices I make for myself, and for my family. Whatever race, nationality, or origin we are, we are pretty much concerned with same things every day. I remember, I once met a German professor who worked as a consultant for our partner company. During our business lunch he turned to me and said: "I think you are one of those 'need to plan everything in advance' type of persons, Asel." When I nodded, he then added: "I am over seventy now. I lived my life without making any plans and being spontaneous, and this helped me to get rid of stress because things do not always go the way we want, as many things are out of our control." On my 2013 resolution list is: "Be spontaneous and worry less!" I hope, this can be fulfilled.

Steve Jobs puts it this way: "Most of our battles we lose in our minds." I tell Dayana when she comes home after school and sits down to do her homework to think only about positive things and be more confident about herself. She shows my type of genes in wanting to know everything in advance, worrying about her math test the next day, planning things ahead all the time, and showing lack of confidence in being able to accomplish a task (in Sciences, for example). Kids learn by examples.

I hope to be showing an example to my child!

Anar shares her challenges and experiences on living in Italy, raising a child, communicating and socializing, interacting with an Italian environment.

Unlike both of my sisters, being business ladies, I have pursued an alternative path in terms of studies and in terms of work. Being the oldest daughter (although my twin sister, Asel, still claims to be the older one, which remains a controversial issue between us) I felt obliged and at the same time very much interested in following in the footsteps of my father. That's why without a second thought I chose international relations as my BA major at the American college in London, followed by a Master's major in the same subject area at American University in Washington, DC.. Upon the completion of the MA, at 21 years old, I thought I was ready to apply in my country the theoretical knowledge I had acquired in the West, and I was impatient to return to Kazakhstan.

The day after the September 11, 2001 terrorist attacks in the US was my very first day at work as a political analyst at the Ministry of Foreign Affairs of Kazakhstan research facility. I will never forget the day I entered the research building for the first time on that day and saw a lot of commotion all around, with people running around the offices, everyone looking concerned and hyperactive. I managed to stop someone and tell him that I was new and it was my first day at work. The man didn't even ask for my name or my ID; he told me to follow him, put me at the desk in front of a computer and only said: "Find all you can that's related to what happened yesterday in the US." This is how I began my work as a researcher for the next 5 years in one of the most turbulent periods in recent human history, for the 9/11 events have significantly altered international relations and the way we view them.

Researching was exciting and interesting; I couldn't be more content. It was at this point though that I was offered to teach a course on International Affairs at an English-speaking University in Almaty, Kazakhstan, given my Western educational background. The teaching experience has entirely convinced me that now it was the path that I wanted to pursue, to engage and interact with students and to help them make sense of the subject. Entering the academic world inevitably meant continuing to study, so that I had to apply for a PhD in my subject area.

In 2009, I was accepted by the PhD program in Political Theory at the LUISS Guido Carli University in Rome. My whole family was as delighted as I was because that meant that I would pursue my studies and at the same time be able to stay with my son, Arlan, who had been living with my parents in Rome since his birth. Without my parent's help in looking after Arlan, I would never have completed the doctoral studies, and for this I am deeply grateful to them for their love, care, and understanding.

In all the countries where I had an opportunity to live and study — the United States, the United Kingdom, Spain — thanks to my father's profession, I always regarded my stay as being temporary. With Italy, it was different. After three years of writing the doctoral thesis on Russian foreign policy, and with the PhD diploma in hand, I found myself in a position as a full-time mother and a wife, discovering that Italy was a perfect place to raise a family. I must admit that I met Gian Marco Sartor at the time when I had least expected to fall in love. Living in Italy is an amazing experience and Italians are a nation with particularities of their own that one gets to discover on the daily basis. They love their country, their language, and their cuisine, and they are very proud of their rich history. To learn the Italian language, the fastest way is undoubtedly to interact directly with Italians. Gian Marco spoke very little English and when I met him I spoke very little Italian. This meant that I had no choice but to learn the language and learn it as fast as I could for I was very motivated to get to know Gian Marco better.

This had happened through simple daily interaction with my future husband, and my strong desire to conquer the language all together. Then, of course, I joined an Italian language course that lasted a month. It really helped me to solidify what I learned through daily interaction, for I had a chance to see the Italian language on paper, how it was written grammatically, its word order, and watch out for those tricky grammatical mistakes that most foreigners made. But, of course, at the end of the day, the Italian spoken on the streets of Rome was not the same as written in language manuals for foreigners.

Speaking Italian in Italy is quintessential; one just can't do without it, be it making friends, dealing with complicated Italian bureaucracy, or signing up your child for a swimming course. Everything entailed speaking Italian, not only because not many in Italy speak English or any other language, but because Italians really sincerely view their language as being very important and expect foreigners to master it, should one choose to live in the country.

For example, at Arlan's English-speaking elementary school, many mothers of other kids in my son's class speak good English and, in the first encounters, we communicated in English and I always felt that we communicated in a rather formal way. One day, one of the mothers of Arlan's classmates asked me how my Italian was and, in reply, I responded in Italian telling her in a few sentences and she became more than excited that I could, in fact, communicate in Italian. From that day on, she has treated me as a good friend, always stopping by to exchange a few words and greet me more warmly than before when I had spoken English with her. I felt the difference right away.

I cannot help but emphasize two important traits of the Italian soul: the way they treat children and Italian cuisine. What really amazes me is how much Italians love children, whether theirs or those of others. Children are pampered in Italy, and this I discovered first-hand with my son, Arlan, who found himself in a surrounding full of love, joy, and care. Everywhere we go — a restaurant, a park, a hair-

dresser, or a grocery store, Arlan gets the attention of the adults in the sweetest ways. One sees kids in Italy screaming, shouting, running around, and no one will ever reprimand them for it.

It's very rare to see a mother punishing or scolding her child in Italy.

Another element to emphasize is how much Italian cuisine is really authentic, rich in variety, and simply delicious! I know that a lot of literature has been written about how great Italian cuisine is, but I cannot help but emphasize it again. Every time we go for lunch or dinner to Gian Marco's parents, we talk a lot about the Italian cuisine. It's actually the main topic at the table; there are endless recipes and thousands of different ways to prepare simple vegetables. Italians take going for groceries and eating out very seriously. In terms of eating out, they are a bit conservative, I would say, as once they find a restaurant of their liking, they continue to go only to this restaurant and become regular clients, which has, of course, its privileges. Regular clients in Italy are treated with lots of care. There is a pizzeria Napolitana where we go every Saturday because Arlan loves their "pizza Margherita con prosciutto cotto e funghi" *and also their* "cotoletta con patatine fritte". *After we had gone there three times, they came to know us and now always give us the best seats and come around to* "fare due chiacchiere", *to chat, to check if what we had ordered was good. Italians value their clients once they become regular.*

Arlan really loves pizza, mozzarella, prosciutto e pasta, only as it is made here in Rome –fresh, tasty, and simply wonderful. What else can a young man growing up ask for? Italian cuisine is unquestionably unbeatable!

Of course, the way Italians treat children and their cuisine are not the only things to emphasize as I continue to discover and learn so many sides to what it means to be Italian and what it means to live in Rome.

They say "When in Rome, do as the Romans do". When St. Augustine asked St. Ambrose to go to Rome on a mission, St. Ambrose became concerned on which holy day to follow, because the Romans fasted on a day that was not his tradition. St. Augustine then advised St. Ambrose wisely, saying "When in Rome, do as the Romans do".

While visiting or living in a foreign country, we might not know customs and traditions of the country but we should definitely follow them, act similar to avoid conflicts and misunderstanding. For my family, living in a foreign environment enriched our perception of the world, gave us and our children an opportunity to assimilate with other cultures, establish relationships with people of different cultural backgrounds, feel comfortable and safe in a host country. Civilization has given us different cultures with the opportunity to learn from each other and to enhance diversity and progress along the way. Cross-cultural observations, abiding by the customs of a society, following basic values while keeping personal identity is the key to a better assimilation into a new, foreign community.

At the same time, each of us has been faced with own experiences, major and minor challenges. Facing challenges has been overwhelming at times and coping with various circumstances has not always been easy.

Some of those challenges helped each of us discover new things about ourselves, playing a role in defining our purpose in life, and each new experience presented lessons to learn from.

CHAPTER VI
SPEAKING OF LANGUAGES

"Language is the skin of the soul."

Fernando Lazaro Carreter

What do we do first when we arrive in a new country? We start learning its language or we do it before our arrival. If not, we may have the sense of isolation caused by not knowing a language around us. For a diplomat at a new posting, not being able to speak easily to people is a critical disadvantage.

Once, there was a driver at our embassy in London who didn't know a word of English. The only thing he knew was the name everyone uses for the giant clock "Big Ben", but even those words he pronounced incorrectly, omitting the last letters of each word, so it became "Bi' Be'". He had been circling around near that famous clock for hours until a traffic policeman noticed his strange maneuvers and stopped him. The driver kept pronouncing those words, and the policeman finally understood what he meant and pointed to the clock high on the tower. Thanking the policeman, the driver smiled that he could now find his way home. That incident probably wouldn't have happened if the driver had known English. Our driver in Belgium signed up for English lessons recently. As we were located in a primarily French part of Belgium, I asked him why English and not French. He answered that English was a universal language. In a practical way, the driver was right. The English language has helped me to adapt to new places, new countries in a smooth way, to work at embassies, talk to local people without interpreters. Wherever we moved, I had a strong desire to learn other languages. By learning the language of a new country, we show respect for its culture, willingness to adapt quicker, a desire to become part of the local scene. It makes our life easier in so many different ways. Besides, learning languages strengthens our mind; it is a gymnastics for our brain.

Language unites people, helping us communicate and share ideas. It is a link throughout the population in an entire country as well as within individual ethnic groups. In Kazakhstan, the state language is Kazakh, while Russian is the language of inter-ethnic communication. In the year of 2007, the policy of a "Trinity of Languages" was introduced in Kazakhstan. The trinity includes Kazakh, Russian, and English. The "Trinity of Languages" project is aimed at the development of multilingual education and support of the state language in all spheres of social life, promotion of its role in strengthening inter-ethnic harmony. However, it is also important to continue using Russian and introduce English, both as the languages of scientific research and international cooperation.

There is a long controversy in my country among real Kazakhs, who are called *nagyz Kazakh*, and Russified Kazakhs (like me), who are sometimes called *semi-Kazakhs* or even *mancurts* (people who have lost their cultural roots). I don't want to get sidetracked in the long process of that controversy because, finally, much of the question is semantic. For example, I don't find the definition of *mancurt* or *semi-Kazakh* very accurate. I have never considered myself to be *semi-Kazakh*. There is semi-fat milk, which has only half the fat of regular milk, and there is semi-sweet chocolate, which has less sweetness than other chocolate. The term "semi" sounds like you are missing something. I don't feel that I am missing anything, but rather my cultural composition is slightly different from that of a nagyz Kazakh. I am a Russified Kazakh because I speak Russian better than Kazakh: I think in Russian, I write in Russian, I speak Russian in full range. I know Kazakh thanks to my late grandmother but my Kazakh is limited. I don't habitually read Kazakh literature, though I admire it. From my point of view, it doesn't matter whether I use Kazakh everyday or not. I am proud I am Kazakh. Whenever I have the chance, I enjoy listening to the TV news in Kazakh. I love Kazakh lyrical songs, and I deeply moved by Abai Kunanbayev's poetry (Kazakh poet and educator, and the father of modern written Kazakh literature), his proverbs, in particular, but also his translation of the great Russian poet Pushkin. The Russian classics had a profound impact on Abai Kunanbayev and he urged our people to acquire a knowledge of Russian culture. This is meant to enrich the Kazakh people, not semi- denature them. Russification happened not only in my case, but a whole generation shifted its native language comprehension because of the language policy of the Soviet Union. To some, understandably, this is a loss, but, to others, there was a gain in another direction, as the Soviet infrastructure opened many new possibilities to the Kazakhs.

Our great poet Abai Kunanbayev once said:

"Language has free will in it and it warms the heart". It warms the heart when we hear foreigners speak Kazakh. I had this unique opportunity to watch two women, one Kazakh, another Dutch, to speak Kazakh. The Dutch woman didn't even have a foreign accent. She was using southern Kazakh dialect. Later I found out she had been living in a Kazakh countryside for several years. Many Russians living in Kazakhstan speak perfect Kazakh. I once attended a party where there was only one Russian woman. She was the only one among Kazakhs who could sing in Kazakh. Shame on us!

In Soviet times Kazakhstan was a very Russified state where Kazakhs didn't even represent a majority of the population, and the Kazakh language was not widely spoken. My generation (1960s-70s) attended Russian schools, and we had only two Kazakh schools in Almaty, the former capital of Kazakhstan (still considered a southern capital). Our parents, having a good command of Kazakh, used to speak both languages in the family: they would address us in Kazakh and we would reply in Russian. That was a common daily situation in almost all families of the Soviet Kazakhstan. It is still common for Kazakhs educated in the Soviet period to speak Kazakh with their elders and people coming from rural areas. The degree to which this is a good thing or a bad thing is a matter of interpretation. Maybe it is not even the right question, as we may simply be talking about the evolution of a society. Evolution doesn't have to be judged as good or bad; it simply reflects the reality of the times. And semi-sweet chocolate does not have to be considered bitter.

Languages always fascinated me. At school during the first four grades, I dreamed of being a doctor. I used to collect newspaper and magazine articles about diseases, and everybody was convinced that I would become a doctor some day. When I became a fifth-grader, we started a new subject: English! Imagine English in the 60s in Kazakhstan. German was more popular than English at that time in Kazakhstan, especially after the Second World War, when East Germany entered the Soviet sphere. There was nothing to read in English, no magazines, a few dictionaries, no foreigners to talk to, and the only newspaper we had was the *Moscow News*, which looked like a normal Soviet paper of that time.

I immediately fell in love with the English language. I was the best in class and actually in school as far as English lessons were concerned. I fell in love with English literature. I began reading everything we had in English in the libraries. So, when it was time to finish high school and choose a university, I made up my mind to enter Almaty Pedagogical Institute of Foreign Languages (now the University of World Languages), the English Department. First, I had to talk to my father as the head of the family, and he said: "No! You will be unemployed. You will not find any job. English is not math or chemistry. Nobody needs it!" And so on and so forth. We had a neighbor, an English teacher, whose husband was my father's friend. She was a university lecturer, and she often brought university students to our high school for their teaching practice. She was struck by my command of English and talked to my father about my language proficiency. He was speechless.

After graduating from the University of Foreign Languages with honors, I couldn't find a job. My father was right. I was now married, and three years passed taking care of our twin babies, which was my first real job, and my big priority. When the children started kindergarten, I finally found a part-time job, which suited me and my family because I had time to manage both the household work and my job. Now I think that if my father hadn't approved of my choice, my major wouldn't have been English. I might have become a doctor with full-time work, and that would have changed my whole approach to raising children. In a real way, language changed my life and the life of my children.

To integrate culturally is to integrate linguistically, I would say, whether at home or abroad. When my daughter Asem finished her studies in London, I came to help her to pack. We went to the Heathrow airport with suitcases: big and small ones, a guitar, and a computer. And all the way to the check-in desk we worried about the overweight of our luggage. A girl at the check-in desk was dealing with our tickets. At that time we lived in Spain and judging by her accent I realized that the girl was Spanish. I asked her if she was from Spain. She nodded her head and I switched into Spanish telling her that my daughter finished her BA and we were going back to Madrid where we lived, and we loved Madrid, which was true. She praised my Spanish and we talked about Spain a bit. She said we had thirty-five kilograms overweight but she let us go without paying for it. She did it because she appreciated our Spanish, our affection towards her country. In this case, a knowledge of a foreign language helped us with the situation. We felt a little guilty, actually, but we also felt almost as though the language made us part of some larger Spanish family.

On another occasion, Asem and I had just returned to Kazakhstan from our posting in Great Britain. At that time, there was the inauguration of the new capital, Astana, Kazakhstan. We were expecting the arrival of many prominent guests to celebrate the festivities. Almaz was busy with foreign delegations, as he was Vice-Minister of Foreign Affairs of Kazakhstan (that's why we had to change our posting in Britain). He gave us invitations to enter the stadium where the main event was supposed to start and asked us not to be late. And we were late. When we reached the stadium, we saw many late people and policemen were letting in only foreigners because they had come the farthest, which in a sense was actually our case. At the entry gate, I showed the policemen our invitations. And to demonstrate that we in fact had come from abroad, Asem spoke to him American English (she actually had an American accent) so the policemen let us in as we had come such a long way to reach Kazakhstan.

Kazakh hospitality is a great thing after all, and knowing a foreign language was the key to our door.

Languages have the unique potential of breaking down barriers between people and countries. One of the CIS ambassadors told us a story which happened to him in Italy. He was driving a car himself and didn't follow the sign when a policeman stopped him. The policeman pointed to the sign and was going to fine the ambassador when the latter said in Italian: "Italy is such a beautiful country that you just miss the signs and everything admiring Italian nature". The policeman struck by the praise of his country and good knowledge of Italian told the ambassador to follow him to the road to his destination. Needless to say, the ambassador never received his fine.

I often recall an episode which happened in Italy with an Ambassadress of a CIS country. During one of the first days of their posting in Italy, when her husband bought a new pair of shoes in Rome, she, being emotional and trying to compliment him, exclaimed: "You look like Domenica Aperto!" In Italian, *domenica* means Sunday, *aperto* open, and she used to see this "Open on Sunday" sign in shops everywhere, so it sounded to her like a famous designer name such as *Roberto Cavalli* or *Sandro Ferrone*. Every time we meet, we laugh about the new famous designer Domenica Aperto.

When we arrived in Spain, I didn't know a word in Spanish. English was not widely understood. For the first time, I felt useless. I felt I was forced to sink or swim. When I went to the post office to send a letter to Kazakhstan, I memorized only one question: *"Donde está el correo?"* (Where is the post office?). When I found the post office, I was interrogated with a battery of questions as to where Kazakhstan was and how I wished to send my letter, and then I was asked to fill in a form with my address in Kazakhstan. Nobody spoke any English at the post-office. I realized I had to learn Spanish to survive in everyday situations. In a few days, I signed up for the course of Spanish together with my daughter in a group of foreigners. And in two years, we got a diploma *"Español para Extranjeros, Nivel Superior"* (Spanish for Foreigners, High Level).

Group learning is challenging. Some people have pronunciation difficulties, others don't understand the structure of the language because of the influence of their native language in relation to the foreign one. I find it interesting to observe the influence of a mother tongue on the second language. It is a natural instinct to look for similarities with things that are familiar, to draw comparisons with what we already know. To some extent, we rely on our mother tongue to learn a foreign language. Language transfer is sometimes called cross- linguistic influence, or interference. Linguists define positive and negative transfers. To learn Spanish, I found it comfortable to use an English-Spanish or a Spanish- English dictionary instead of Russian-Spanish or Spanish- Russian. English and Spanish as languages are cousins, as they have common ancestors in Latin and Greek, while Russian, being a Slavic language, is on a different branch of the Indo-European family. I remember that some Russian girls in our group asked for my dictionary that I had in the class, and when they saw it was Spanish- English dictionary, they were surprised to know I was using English instead of Russian. Our brain works by making associations. I almost irritated an Italian teacher when I would notice similarities between Italian and English, for example. "Oh, this word sounds English!" I would make my own discoveries and it helped me to memorize words in association with English. Perhaps the Italian teacher, like some linguists, believed that it is best to learn a language without any attempt to translate back and forth from one language to another, to avoid negative transfers (confusion). But in my experience, any way of learning languages has advantages and disadvantages. As the Spanish say: *Lo que no se va en lágrimas va en suspiros* (what you don't lose in tears you lose in sighs).

In any case, learning a foreign language is a long process. In everyday practice, we need to be understood and nobody will wait for us to adapt to the new environment linguistically. In this case, patterns are helpful. At the beginning common phrases are easy to follow, like: *"I need an appointment with a doctor"* (a banker, a secretary, a teacher,…), *"Where is a* train station?" (a pharmacy, a bus stop, a bathroom,…), *"I would like* pasta " (red wine, water, grilled fish,…), *"Could you, please,* call me back?" (spell your name, give me your phone number, fill in this paper,…), *"I want you to* send me a message (call the office, come earlier, sign in,…), and so on. Then of course we can go from easy structures to complex ones.

Later I attended a course organized by renowned Spanish University Complutense of Madrid on Spanish

History and Culture, entitled "Spain in the 20th century", "Spain: history, geography, society and culture" for wives of ambassadors accredited in Spain. After completing the course, we also received a diploma. We did not have a high level of Spanish, but the lectures were held in standard Castilian Spanish and were quite comprehensible to all of us no matter what level of Spanish we had. It gave us a good sense of progress and achievement, and of course encouragement to continue learning the language.

I remember my first serious experience with the Spanish language. When I became the vice-president of *Damas Diplomáticas* (a diplomatic association of wives of ambassadors and diplomats accredited in Spain) we held our meetings in Spanish, since that was the language of the association, rather than English, as is usual in a group of all foreigners. The president of the association at that time was Marie Van de Ross, wife of ambassador of South Africa (the term for the president was two years). It was the beginning of my second year in Spain and I began using Spanish. As for Marie, she didn't speak Spanish at all. She started a meeting in English and immediately complaints were voiced by other board members. They were mainly from Latin American countries, so they demanded to speak Spanish. I intervened by asking them to be patient and give us time to learn Spanish. Marie got a bit ruffled but continued the meeting in English. She just didn't have any option. After the meeting, Marie told me she would bring her husband's secretary next time to help her with the translation.

In a month, right before the following meeting, Marie called me to say that she wouldn't be able to come to the meeting because she was busy with the guests from South Africa and asked me to hold the meeting instead of her. I didn't sleep a night before the meeting because I was so nervous, and I was sure I wouldn't be able to express myself to my complete ability in Spanish. I always panic this way –worrying too much trying to make things perfect. While panicking, I began to work on my speech. I made a list of all possible Spanish words I might use and they might ask me on the subject and wrote down their translation into English. I also prepared some useful phrases, introductory words and even proverbs and sayings. Now you can imagine board members' reaction when I started speaking Spanish; at that moment, I felt they didn't expect me to complete my mission "impossible". But they were pleasantly surprised, and that was an encouraging start for me.

They say, "live and learn", and this is true when you use what you learn in everyday situations in a foreign environment. In Spanish the phrase *"la semana que viene"* would mean "next week". There are many situations where you might ask to set up an appointment with your dentist for next week or ask a professor to meet you for additional lecture the following week. Our daughter Asel, who was living with us in Madrid and studying towards her MBA degree at the local American International University in Spain missed her lecture session with one of the Spanish professors because they had different definitions of the word "next". The professor referred to *"lunes que viene"* meaning "this coming Monday", but Asel understood it to mean "next Monday" and showed up for class a week after it was actually scheduled. We will never forget the danger of misinterpreting the concept "next" in Spanish, which was fixed in our minds forever. Asel was thankful for the opportunity to learn Spanish, since most of their lecturers were locally hired professors who had mastered of English to some degree, but switched very often from English to their native Spanish. This switching back and forth between languages is called code switching, which can be a source of richness, when constructions or words from one language are used because they may not exist in the other language. Or it can simply be the easiest way to express an idea when the speaker does not know one of the languages well. Code switching can irritate purists, who may show their disdain for a hybrid of English and Spanish by calling it "Spanglish". In the classroom environment, this code switching was meant to help students comprehend the subject, but some lecturers switched from English entirely to Spanish, insisting that, as Spanish is spoken in many parts of the world, the international student body should take advantage of the opportunity and learn the local language properly. But the courses were supposed to be taught only in English, so many students did complain that professors tried to make their own life easier by lecturing in their native language. Each culture has its own way of praising its native language.

I will definitely never forget the long Spanish word *"ininterrumpidamente"* ("continuously, without a break") because usually everything in Spain closes up from 13:00

to 16:00 and also because it is not easy to pronounce it. I have this ability to memorize difficult and irrelevant words, while easy words don't attract my attention. They say that "antidisestablishmentarianism" is the longest word in English (biochemists would disagree), but what good did this word ever do anyone?

In Italy I immediately joined the course of the Italian language on a private basis. Whereas in Spain I had attended language courses with a group of other foreigners, this time in Italy I made up my mind to have private lessons for only three months to learn the basic structure of the Italian language. I asked my teacher to tailor the program to my needs to be able to speak Italian as soon as possible, to practice dialogues with the teacher, to learn a few of the local expressions, to get results by using a language for communication, let's say, in the pharmacy to get medicine, at the bakery to buy bread, at embassy receptions to introduce myself, and to say a few polite words wherever the circumstance might arise. Later, I joined a conversation class with other ambassadresses accredited to the Italian Republic. In a relatively short time, I had a basic working knowledge of the language. Nevertheless, I noticed that whenever I addressed Italians in their language and made myself clear, they spoke English to me, and in this way they tried to get some practice in English, but I tried to stick to Italian to have some practice too. So, at first, with all the switching back and forth, I didn't get all the practice I expected to get.

Learning a language that is close to one you already know seems as though it should be easy, but it can present unforeseen problems. Once, I almost got irritated when ordering a cake for my granddaughter at our local *pasticceria* (pastry shop) in Rome. I made myself understood with the help of the Spanish language and gestures, but when they asked me what date I needed the cake to be done, I said in Spanish instead of Italian: *dieciocho*. They looked at me as if I used a very bad word. I repeated, but no reaction. I got confused. At that moment it didn't come to my mind to write the number down. To my relief, a woman who entered the pastry shop heard me repeating the word and she explained to the attendant that I meant "eighteen". Later, I learned that in Italian "eighteen" is *diciotto*. For me, the difference between the Spanish and Italian words was minimal, but then in English, there is a minimal difference between the sound of the words fifteen and fifty. Sometimes it seems that people don't try hard enough to understand a foreigner, but in fact the problem comes when pronunciation passes a threshold of understanding, like the minor difference between "do" and "two". A Spaniard might pronounce the sentence "I see you" as "Ice eat chew" and wonder why an Englishman returns a blank look. The possibilities of misunderstanding are infinite.

For eight years in Italy we used to go to one and the same beach. It was a local Italian beach in Fregene, which was only half an hour drive from our home. There were two changing rooms with showers for men and women. The signs on doors were almost alike with a slight difference of the last letter: *Signori/Signore*. At first, before entering, it took us seconds to remember that *Signori* meant men and *Signore* women. Later, we just used to enter automatically. And I thought about foreigners who might get confused as we did at first.

It is better not to feel embarrassed or to be afraid of making mistakes when trying to speak a foreign language. And if we make mistakes, it is normal; it is an attempt to improve and an opportunity to laugh. Laughter is often a very bonding experience. After the pastry shop experience, when we solved the crisis of the word "eighteen", we all laughed, and afterwards, whenever I went into that pastry shop, they were especially friendly to me.

Speaking a foreign language in the country where no one would expect you to speak language can also lead to unexpected circumstances. People may say things in front of you that they normally would not say, thinking that you do not understand. I'm sure this must have happened also to the Dutch lady in Kazakhstan who spoke a local dialect. My Asian looks have advantages when I speak Russian. People often speak foreign languages in front of me as though I am a child and will not understand adult talk, and sometimes it embarrasses them when I respond in their own language. And, in fact, we did exactly that to hide something from our grandchildren when they were small and didn't know foreign languages. And from time to time, they surprised us, too. Now they know too much, so it's almost impossible to hide adult discussions from them by using a language they don't know. These days, the only secretive use I have for language is the selection of Kazakh letters for my credit card pin in Belgium. I hope crooks are as innocent as my grandchildren used to be.

In the beginning, I mixed both languages, especially when the words were very similar, using the Spanish *siempre* instead of the Italian *sempre* (meaning "always" in both languages). Sometimes the differences in pronunciation caused quizzical looks: *fuera* in Spanish *fuori* in Italian (both meaning "outside"). More serious problems (negative transfers) came in mixing up words that looked and sounded similar but had quite different meanings. For instance, in Spanish *salir* means "to leave", while in Italian *salire* means "to go up". I am fully aware that, in my case, the foreign languages that were not developed from a very young age required practice and social interaction with native speakers, and only that would help me to integrate to be able to express myself and be understood.

In Belgium I also signed up for language courses, this time French and German. A real challenge. To my delight, I do not mix them as they are so different. It would be much more difficult if I learned French and Italian at the same time, I think. At first, I thought I would join a class with a group of foreigners. Later I realized I needed private lessons *tête-à-tête* to go deeply into these languages. Language learning requires huge effort but it opens so many doors. What a joy to be able to utter a word in a foreign language, make up a sentence, or get the meaning of the word! For instance, German is a language of compound words. My German teacher patiently asks me to play with the words to find the root of the word, analyze its composition in order to come to a grammar rule intuitively. I found a real treasure:

Mehrwertsteuerrückerstattung (the V.A.T. refund office; I'm still working on the etymology).

Emperor Charles V allegedly said: "I speak Spanish to God, Italian to women, French to men, and German to my horse". I am not an emperor but I get satisfaction being able to speak to a Spaniard in Spanish, an Italian in Italian, an American or British person in English, a Russian in Russian, a Kazakh in Kazakh, and hopefully soon a French speaker in French, and a German speaker in German. Perhaps I would speak Kazakh to my horse, if I had one, as Kazakh people are such excellent horse trainers. In any case, I admire people who speak several languages fluently. A good example is Irene Koch, my best friend, her husband Thomas, and their son Jonas. She is American and Thomas is German and Jonas was born in Germany but spent most of his childhood in Spain. They switch from English to German, and from German to Spanish with such ease that if you heard them without knowing them, you might not know whether they are three Spaniards, three Germans, or three Americans. They told me they used to have Spanish, English, and German days in their family.

Our family has a similar mixture. Our daughters speak several foreign languages: Anar speaks English and Italian, Asel English, Spanish, and German, Asem English, Italian, Spanish, and German (and she can even differentiate between the dialects of Spanish and German). Asem is proud of speaking Russian without a foreign accent. Our grandchildren, after finishing the first grade in Russian started English and Italian. They are both at the stage of switching from one language to another and mixing words. The other day our grandson Arlan said: *Voglio swimming!* (*voglio* is *I want* in Italian). Sounds more Italian than English, to my mind. Our grandson living in an Italian environment acquired typical Italian pronunciation when a short vowel sound ending in English is affixed with a consonant, because most Italian words end with a vowel. Italians give full value or emphasis to all syllables and this results in the stereotypical Italian production of sentences that sound Italian, not English. Italian is a syllable-timed language (syllables tend to follow each other at regular intervals, with an equal amount of time being allocated for each syllable), English is stress-timed (stresses tend to occur at regular intervals and the remaining unstressed syllables, no matter how many in number, have to be squeezed in between the stresses to accommodate the regular beat of the stress). Moreover, when speaking Russian, our grandson does the same with Russian endings, and that's why phonetically his Russian sentence sounds more Italian than Russian.

When English words are used commonly in Italian, it is called Anglitaliano, the Italian answer to Spanglish or Franglais, for example. There is also Itanglese as opposed to Anglitaliano. In Italy, there is a common use of the English words: *il weekend, lo stress, lo shopping, okay, il wedding planner, no comment, il personal trainer, lo spelling, FAQ (frequently asked questions), il fitness*, and so on. I was surprised to know, for instance, that in Spain the word for computer is *ordenador*, not computer, although in Mexico, the tendency is to use *computadora*. The same with French *ordinateur*. The scope of English word usage in Russian is also broad. Words such as *drive, promotion, wow, cool, device, developer, street view, shopping* and so forth are widely used in Russian. Languages develop and become more international.

In the States, when Asem studied at primary school, I insisted on her going to the Russian embassy school three times a week, as I was afraid she might lose her Russian. It was hard for her to attend both schools. She memorized Russian verses with great difficulty, made terrible grammar and spelling mistakes. I couldn't leave her by herself with that big burden, so we did her homework together. I learned the same verses to support her, kept reading in Russian aloud for her to avoid being bored, simplified sentences, and explained grammar rules.

At the same time, I made friends with some mothers whose kids went to the American school. When we had birthday parties with Russian children, they used to speak English instead of Russian! Later adults got tired of driving kids to both schools. We were among the few who kept taking Russian classes in the afternoon. In a couple of years Asem was able to read *Anna Karenina* in original! Now she understood that, had we quit Russian at the beginning, she might have developed a foreign accent when speaking Russian. She also understood that attending both schools made her more organized, flexible, and hard-working.

Some people do not acquire foreign-language fluency even after ten or fifteen years' residence in a host country. They learn just enough simple expressions in a broken foreign language to make themselves understood, but never go any further. There are a number of reasons for this. In many instances I have found that people who know they will spend, for example, only two years in a country think it is not worth putting in all that effort, time, and money into learning a language of a temporary place of residence. Many people just do not enjoy learning languages and if their job does not depend on it, they would rather take up a hobby or a sport. Many people choose simply to get by with English. English is spoken by many across the globe and some feel it is enough. Staying in that comfort or safety zone of a language, at any level, is called fossilizing. Going beyond that level can feel threatening. But sometimes refusing to go beyond a rudimentary level may simply be negligence. And negligence towards the foreign language, I think, can be the negligence towards the culture of the country they live in. Goethe was even harsher in his appraisal: "Those who know nothing of foreign language know nothing of their own."

During the Soviet times in Kazakhstan, people were used to a different grading system on foreign-language proficiency with "I speak English (or other foreign language) well" or "English with the help of the dictionary" often written on a job application paper. Let's examine this system. Imagine you are in the queue to buy oranges, for example. When it is your turn, you take out a dictionary and look for a word *an orange*. Then you search the word *price*. It might take less time if you know the English alphabet, because, if not, you will never get oranges. English with the help of a dictionary may spell hunger.

Many years ago I came across a wonderful book of Hungarian linguist Kato Lomb "How I Learn Languages". Kato knew sixteen languages. The following quotations from her book might help to learn more about languages: "Well-intentioned sentences full of mistakes can still build bridges between people". This comment is a good way to keep people from feeling demoralized.

"The most secure and painless way to the perfect mastery of, let's say, German is being born a German". This comment is a good way to keep people feeling demoralized. Every year since February 2000 International Mother Language Day is observed to promote linguistic and cultural diversity and multiculturalism and multilingualism. This year the theme of the International Mother Day is *Mother Tongue Instruction and Inclusive Education*. UNESCO highlights the importance of the mother tongue as part of the right to education and encourage its member states to promote instruction and education in the mother tongue. Inclusion in education is an approach to educating students with special educational needs. Languages are the most powerful instruments of preserving and developing our tangible and intangible heritage. It is important to develop fuller awareness of linguistic and cultural traditions throughout the world and to inspire solidarity based on understanding, tolerance, and dialogue.

If only I could, I would create a unique language with the perfect English word order, rich Russian vocabulary, Italian expressive rhythm, French mellifluous sound, German word economy, Latin proverbs, Kazakh vowel harmony, Spanish idiomatic expressions. Now, if I could just learn all the other three thousand languages in the world, maybe I could perfect this unique language!

By learning foreign languages, we gain new horizons, widen our communication and thinking abilities, reinforce our own identity and our self-confidence. Every language is unique, and being able to practice a new language gives us access to another culture. It is a challenge to develop.

CHAPTER VII
THINKING AND RETHINKING EDUCATION

"Education is simply the soul of a society asit passes from one generation to another."

G.K.Chesterson

"What do you do at school, Asem?" I used to ask our eight-year-old daughter when she entered John Eaton Elementary School in Washington, D.C..

"We sing, play flute, dance, jump in the school yard," she would usually reply.

"How about math?" I would keep asking her about a new school.

"Oh, Miss Fessenden said I am a wonder kid! I know the whole multiplication table!"

Asem started school in Kazakhstan. She was a calm, responsible child. She would come from kindergarten and tell us she has been praised by a kindergarten teacher. We would ask her what for. And she would tell us "for being silent!" Asem finished her first school year having learnt the whole multiplication table by heart, and this was the time we moved to the USA.

I realized I had to talk to Miss Fessenden. I called a school office and asked for the appointment with Asem's class teacher, a pleasant young woman we met the first day at school. Asem started school with no English and the first two months she had been learning English. In two months time, Miss Fessenden told us, Asem didn't need any extra English classes. So, she could join the whole class and concentrate more on other subjects. But our daughter kept telling us about singing, dancing, playing as if they had been studying in a music conservatory.

I asked Miss Fessenden if Asem was coping with the school subjects. She said that Asem was a bright student, a wonder child because she knew the multiplication table by heart, she solved math problems in her head without a calculator. I was surprised students were allowed to use a calculator. "What if a calculator goes dead?" I asked her.

"Buy a new one!" She answered.

Miss Fessenden noticed my concern and explained that kids should feel comfortable at school, and should enjoy school and the process of learning. That's why the first-grade students wrote with pencils instead of pens, used calculators, changed their seats whenever they wanted, had more breaks to relax, and were given no homework. When I asked Asem if she liked going to school, she had her own explanation: "Today Miss Fessenden asked me if I wanted to clean a blackboard, and I said, 'No, I don't.'" She just didn't want to clean the board. Why should she clean the board if she was given a chance not to do it? Asem is not lazy, she just used another option, that's all.

I'll never forget how we came to school on the first day of classes. By that time we already knew that nobody took flowers to teachers to congratulate them on the first school day of the year. In Kazakhstan, students go to school, especially the first graders, with a lot of excitement. Schools are decorated with balloons and flowers, students put on new black and white uniforms, girls look more attractive because of big ribbons in their hair, and everybody carries a bouquet of flowers. All the students, carrying their backpacks, are accompanied by parents and grandparents. On the small square at the school entrance, there is a short meeting followed by the first bell rung by a high-school student and a first grader together.

In any case, we went to John Eaton Elementary public school beforehand not to miss anything. We didn't see any excitement in the eyes of the students. It didn't look like the first day of the school: students came in their casual outfits. There were a few moms, mainly with the small kids. We had been waiting for the teachers, and not the other way around. Teachers appeared a few minutes before the bell rang. One teacher came in a T-shirt, slapped hands with the students and they filed into the class. I saw disappointment in Asem's eyes. There was no excitement on the first school day abroad.

Our twin daughters, in ninth grade, went to the local school, Woodrow Wilson High School in Washington, D.C.. At the school entrance, two black school guards were searching the students, looking for drugs and weapons. Students were then gathered in the school assembly room, where the school principal welcomed newcomers and greeted the students on their first school day. Our girls had been given a choice of subjects, and they chose chemistry only for one semester, and chose among other lessons such as Creative Writing, Visual Arts, History, Drama, PE (physical exercises), Algebra, English Enrichment, Biology, Geography. The history of District of Columbia was taught for the whole semester. By the end of that semester Anar and Asel could name every senator ever elected in D.C..

They were also obligated to do hundred hours of community service in addition to their studies (otherwise they wouldn't graduate from school). Asel chose to work in the library, and Anar assisted her English professor. This was done a bit differently in Kazakhstani schools and usually took a voluntary form in helping elderly shop for groceries, cross streets, and walk their pets, or collect paper for recycling, look for and submit metal scraps for reprocessing, or taking care of the trees in the school yard.

In our schools in Kazakhstan, many things have changed but school subjects have remained basically the same. It is obligatory to have math, physics, and chemistry, and the level of teaching is high. I remember how we learned geography when I was a schoolgirl. We memorized, for example, the names of big and small rivers in the US, all of its states with capitals, not to mention the European countries, their climate zones, direction of winds, and the names of mountains and bays, straits, rivers, and tributaries. In chemistry class, we were supposed to know the whole Mendeleyev periodic table of elements. In math, we were taught high math. We were definitely overloaded with the mass of information, and not everything remained in our memory, but it remained as a base, anyway.

Our granddaughter Dayana, after having spent seven and a half years in Italy with us went back to Kazakhstan and her parents enrolled her in Miras International School in Astana, Kazakhstan. Overall, Dayana's school is a blend of local policies and internationally accepted standards of education, mainly those of the US. Even though the primary school that our granddaughter attends in Kazakhstan is an international school, some school policies that were in force even in our times when we were back in school are still being applied. Neat and correct writing, for example, greatly influences the child's grade. Teachers often correct children on their postures during classes and pay close attention to how well children wash their hands after a meal, and after brunch they walk in the school yard. Kids are not allowed to sit on the floor without mats as opposed to sitting anywhere and without any mats in US, for example. Our grandson, being a neat boy, has difficulty sitting on the floor because it is not clean enough for him. I remember I used to bring a mat for Asem in Washington, D.C.. She was the only one with the mat and it didn't bother her. My grandmother used to warn me not to sit on something cold, as it could harm a woman's health, she used to say, especially during delivery. I always trusted my grandma and passed her experience to my daughters, and now to our grandchildren.

Recently, while visiting my daughter and grandson, who attended Rome International School, I met his teacher, Miss Tigani. She was telling us about Arlan's progress in all subjects, including English. This school managed to put foreign students in special classes to get them used to the language first before transferring them to regular classes. Arlan felt comfortable in English class as he was the only foreign student in his grade when he started the school. Miss Tigani also stressed that Arlan was enjoying school and it was obvious as he willingly attended school even if his English was not fluent. At the same time, discipline and responsibility taught by Miss Svetlana Nesterova at the Russian Embassy School in Rome during his first grade helped our grandson to do his best in making progress. We will always be grateful to those teachers who dedicate their time and effort to our children.

Children learn how to treat others from how they are treated themselves. The Golden Rule. Of course, they like to be praised and encouraged. I like the way kids are praised abroad in the superlative degree: "Great!", "Fantastic!", "Incredible!", "Perfect!", "Terrific!", "Wonderful!" Even we adults feel much better if we are praised for speaking foreign languages. "Prima!" says my German teacher when I do not confuse the *Dativ* and Akkusativ cases.

In Kazakh culture, to my mind, children are more spoilt than praised. Instruction is given in an imperative way, and kids are loaded with homework and after-school activities. Teamwork is appreciated more than individuality. The word of a teacher is final and indisputable, at least in primary school. Discipline and self-discipline are priorities in our schools, as it was thirty or forty years ago.

Modern private schools today in Kazakhstan are more relaxed in terms of discipline and teamwork. For teachers in private schools it is difficult to deal with the children of the Kazakh elite, many of whom are not used to discipline at all. Some students have personal drivers and bodyguards. Luckily, this is not common.

Western education came into high demand among rich Kazakhs. For those who couldn't afford to study abroad a fully funded government program has been launched. In 1993, Kazakhstan was the first Central Asian country to start a presidential scholarship program "*Bolashak*" to study abroad. *Bolashak* means "the future" in Kazakh, best described as Kazakhstan's recognition of the importance of educating its most talented youth at the best universities of the world, thus enabling them to acquire necessary skills to lead the country into its prosperous future. Upon completion of their programs, scholarship recipients return to Kazakhstan to perform government service for a period of five years. Most Kazakhstan students are sent to be trained in the United States, "to learn from the positive examples of American democracy", said our President. More than 400 students are graduates of the leading US universities, such as Harvard, Massachusetts Institute of Technology, Georgetown, Duke, and many others.

Children remember selectively, as we all do. They are more attuned to the present than the past or the future. We left abroad when our youngest, Asem, was eight years old. She does not remember the time spent in Kazakhstan before our departure to the US. She remembers it only through our stories. At first, I thought it happened because she had more impressions about the United States than Kazakhstan, where her life had been more stable and routine. Then I realized (I might be wrong) we did not talk to her about our daily experiences when we lived in Kazakhstan. We all lived through future expectations, dreaming and making plans. By the way, Asem forgot the whole multiplication table by the end of the first year at the American school because she did not need it, having a calculator.

We often remind our grandchildren what our country is, where it is situated, what countries Kazakhstan borders on, where we live now, what Italy, for instance, is famous for, what language they speak, and we talk about our plans for a week, talk about our future vacation. Asem, their aunt, is their Geography teacher whenever she visits us. She used to teach them geography with the help of a globe we had in the house. At three, they would name the continents, European and Asian countries, oceans and seas, and differentiate between human races. Their moms would teach them math and reading. And I would teach the children crafts. As soon as Dayana started painting, she would usually sign her painting as I always did, writing down her name, a date and a name of the country. She would tell me: "You can keep it or sell it to get money for poor and disabled kids!"

Almaz is a knowledgeable nature explorer, so he would take the children for walks and tell them about nature, calling their attention to leaves and trunks, and animals and their behavior. We caught a hedgehog in our garden. Almaz bought a turtle for kids, and they gave her a simple name: *Tartaruga* ("Turtle" in Italian). He caught birds and butterflies, and other types of little animals to teach grandchildren to care for them. After a while, feeling pity for those creatures, the children would let them crawl away or fly out of the cage .

Our house, wherever we lived, was a haven for pets. It was Asem's dream to have a dog and we got one in Spain. It was a cocker spaniel with a rare combination of colors — black and white — so we named it Grey. He still lives with us, though he is now old and deaf and has cataracts. In the US, we bought a cockatiel, a medium- sized parrot-like bird. A smart creature, it used to eat everything except its own food. It was given a Kazakh name, *Ak Tirnak*, meaning "White Claw", as it had one white claw. Like our grandchildren, it was very fond of our national Kazakh pasta food. The cockatiel moved with us to the UK, where it flew away when the window was open. In Italy, Dayana got another pet for her birthday,

Indonesian multicolored parrot. We all thought it was a female as the parrot was aggressive and accepted food only from Almaz. It got an Italian name *Capa* which meant a "Head, Boss". Dayana used to play with her parrot and dreamed of making her own show. In a while, almost everybody, including Dayana, lost interest in the parrot. Almaz was the only one in the family who really cared for the birds after all. He used to spoil our grandchildren and now animals. The parrot had several cages: from round to square, from small to big, for travelling, for sleeping at night. The dog was fed three times a day and was given sweet bones and watermelon as treats. Capa turned out to be a male. We had to leave it with our friends when we left for Brussels.

Our grandchildren, like all children, like fairytales, especially Russian ones, where good always wins over bad. Our grandchildren are familiar with world fairytales as well, though some of Hans Christian Andersen's fairytales upset them deeply. Let's take, for example, "A Girl with Matches". A poor barefoot girl dies after failing to sell matches in winter. Our kids cried when they heard her story. Another story was about a poor family with many kids and there was not enough food for everybody, so the parents decided to take them to the forest and leave them there. The youngest, smart son found his way back. Then came the horrible part of the story: the parents took their kids to the forest for the second time! We never went back to that story as our kids got frightened. It wasn't a story where the children were loved and cared for. It might be advisable for parents to read fairytales first, to avoid traumatizing their children. I'm not sure whether gory tales like Hansel and Gretel, where wicked witches fatten up innocent children to eat them, are the best for a tender mind.

Once in Italy, our driver was looking for a cat for his daughters. He went to the pet shop and was given an adoption form which he started filling in. Besides his personal information, he was asked to answer the following questions:

Reason for adoption: for companionship, for love, for a child, for a company for another animal, as a gift, to catch mice.

Are you able to assume responsibility for the care, protection and love of an animal for all of its life up to possibly 20 years?

Who will have primary responsibility for the care of the cat?

What floor do you live on; do you have a garden? Outside the garden is there a lot of traffic? Will the cat be allowed to live in the house?

Is anyone in your family allergic to cats?

Do you promise to have the cat, male or female, sterilized as soon as it is possible to do so?

Do you consent to periodic calls from us to check on the welfare of the animal?

If you move will you take the cat with you?

What will you do with the cat when you are on vacation?

For whatever reason and whenever, if you can no longer keep the cat you pledge to return said cat to us.

Remember to come back to us for advice and information.

Finally, when he handed the form back, the shop-assistant said that since the driver was from the embassy, which meant he was staying in the country for a temporary time, he could not have the cat. Upset by the failure to get a cat for his daughters, the driver picked up an abandoned cat from the street.

Working for an embassy, representing the country we are from always gives us the sense of belonging to our community, following community standards. Kazakhstani diplomats abroad usually do not live in compounds. Our embassy personnel have a choice to find housing according to the budget of his or her diplomatic position. This way our embassy people have opportuni- ty to socialize with foreigners, observe the culture of the host country and learn the language quicker. Also, our diplomats consider school facilities if they have children and receive a certain stipend that partially pays for that education.

Unfortunately, our postings are not organized so that you arrive at the end of summer, like some foreign embassies do, in time for children to start the new school year. This would save time, and would give families with children the possibility of adapting better and preparing for school in the new environment.

The average age of our diplomats abroad is twenty-five to thirty-five years old. Their kids have a choice to attend either local or international schools, or American or Russian embassy schools. It is up to them to make a choice. Some kids go to local schools and attend Russian embassy schools two to three times a week. Others go to local schools where classes are given in Dutch, Italian, Spanish, Flemish, and other languages not common to find in Kazakhstan. When these children return to our country, they face the problem of being far behind their classmates in many subjects, especially languages. Some parents feel that time is lost this way. Other parents are proud that their kids are almost foreigners in their own country. Perhaps the focus should be on the children, who should always feel comfortable, not vulnerable, in the situations they are forced into. If the decisions are made considering the needs of the children and parents together, the situation is more likely to work out, and school education may stay with them a lifetime.

When we moved from the US to the UK, it was almost the end of the school year, Easter break. Asem was angry with us, as if we had had an option and made a bad decision. The twins, on the contrary, were excited that they had missed schooling. Since they all had started their foreign schooling in the US, we decided to stick to the American system of education. But in the American school in London, at almost the end of the school year, there were no vacancies for our children. We were put in a waiting list. Upon arrival in London, we had to live in a multi-storeyed block of flats for a couple of months while we were looking for a house rather than apartment, which was a quarter of an hour walking distance to Buckingham Palace.

Having no time to search for an appropriate school for Asem, I took her to the nearest state school, and I found out that the school was actually for immigrants: Indian, Pakistani girls were wearing scarves and national clothes and speaking their own language. Asem, fluent in American English, was far ahead of the class in many subjects. She got bored.

In two months, we moved to East Sheen, London and I started calling schools in our area to accept our eleven-year-old daughter. They referred me to the local education authorities. I called the office and they said they couldn't accept our daughter in the middle of the school year. I didn't give up and started explaining our situation. I explained that we arrived in Great Britain to build a Kazakhstani-British relationship, that it was not our fault to come late for school, and so on and so forth. There was a pause in the receiver, and the person I had been talking to suggested that I write down what I had just said, including the part about the relationship between Kazakhstan and the United Kingdom of Great Britain and Ireland. I sent my letter, written on an official embassy paper the same day, and in three days I got the reply from them about our daughter's acceptance to the school, which was just behind our house.

More than ten years passed since our daughters graduated from different schools –Kazakhstani, Russian, American, British, public and private. I was pondering what kind of education was the best for our children and grandchildren while listening to the speeches at the public hearing at European Economic and Social Committee Section for Employment, Social Affairs and Citizenship on February, 5th, 2013 in Brussels. The theme of the discussion was "Rethinking Education: Investing in skills for better socio-economic outcomes". The speakers were discussing vocational and traditional education, validation of formal and non-formal learning, the issues of the lack of skills, the unemployment rate in Europe, the Finnish education system, language and computer skills, teachers, and holistic approaches to rethinking education. Meanwhile, I was thinking that generations change, new notions appear but the essence of education remains the same: to provide children with knowledge to gain an enlightening experience. Now the term is to "invest" in a child's education. I was also convinced that we did the right thing in having invested in our daughters' education. We created possibilities for them to learn, offered options to choose from, and, if this financial term is meaningful, we invested in their future.

Having studied at various schools and universities, our daughters were at the same time exposed to diverse cultural environments, and that had significant impact on their life experience. The fact is that cross- cultural learning that comes from traveling and living in diverse places highly enrich one's soul, boost further knowledge acquired from textbooks, help develop further communication skills, and greatly enlarge one's vision about our world at large. My whole family has been blessed with the opportunity to experience a life of a true nomad, an experience that had its difficulties and challenges we had to face up to, the various stages of adaptation and some degree of disappointment at times. Overall, however, exposure to diverse environments has been positive and a very enriching education in the larger sense, creating an immense amount of accumulated experience and knowledge for us.

CHAPTER VIII
A SENSE OF BELONGING

"Patriotism is your conviction that thiscountry is superior to all other countriesbecause you were born in it."

George Bernard Shaw

There was a popular Russian song we used to listen to and sing at our school. It sounds very patriotic and sentimental at the same time but it expresses the feelings you might have towards your own country. It says that "motherhood begins with your alphabet pictures, friends around you, songs your mother used to sing…". It goes on to say that motherhood is where your mother is, where you started your education and environment with friends and family. Almost all of us remember the name of our first teacher, we go back to the favorite places of our childhood, we look for classmates on the Internet, and have class reunions every ten years. We attend the cemetery where our dearest people rest in peace. All of this makes you feel at home, secure, with a sense of belonging. All of this makes you feel emotionally connected to what we call our history and culture. All of this makes you feel that you belong to a country. Feeling that you are part of a homeland means first of all identifying oneself with the country in a unique way.

Defining national identity is hard enough for any country, and Kazakhstan is no exception, particularly because it is a multinational country. We lived through a transition to a market economy, building a new country from scratch. Big steps and little steps were taken to forge democratic development, and it took us only about twenty years to move steadily from a country rich in minerals and oil, but not yet fully developed, to a stable country with vast opportunities and readiness for progress. "If modern-day Kazakhstan is at ease with its past, it faces somewhat of a challenge when it comes to establishing its national identity and solidifying it for its future."[3] The modern and developing Kazakhstan needs to create a strong national identity in order to make sure that it remains on the world map as a nation of its own. Undoubtedly a lot has been achieved so far in all areas of development of the state, society, and economy in a considerably short period of time. The achievements have also been made in foreign policy as the country has been quite active on a regional and international scale. One manifestation is how much the foreign services have been expanded with a growing number of embassies and consulates of Kazakhstan around the world. Kazakhstan has

---

[3] P.37 Claude Salhani. Islam Without a Veil. Kazakhstan's Path of Moderation.

put forward its own notion of tolerance of other ethnicities and religions. The ethnic makeup of the Kazakhstan society is very diverse, more than 120 nationalities represented. Thus it was essential to promote a policy of interethnic consensus based on the principle for internal stability widely recognized in the world. In terms of religion, there are about 3000 religious unions representing more than 40 confessions in Kazakhstan. After the country gained independence the policy on religious practices has been radically changed from that of Soviet period, during which there was a widespread discrimination against religious groups. The government has adopted laws granting full freedom of religion and has started promoting the idea of spiritual accord and inter-confessional cooperation. For decades it has stood at the forefront of promoting this essential notion. The government promotes a sense of national homeland meant to unite peoples regardless of their ethnic, religious and national origin. This is undoubtedly significant for the region of Central Asia as well as the world at large. It is heartening that Kazakhs are not among the immigrants fleeing the country in search of work, though our ancestors were nomads leaving one pasture for another in search of food for cattle and a better place for living. You hardly see our people abroad looking for a place to live or a job to do. It is also our tradition to live where you were born.

On the other hand, I am not happy or proud when I meet Kazakh *nouveau riche* with lots of money without knowing how to spend it wisely. They are those, to my mind, with a kind of autism, living in a social bubble. They

The first thing most foreigners associate with Kazakhstan is oil. We are repeatedly called an "oil-rich country". But not everybody knows that Kazakhstan exports hard grain to many countries, including Russia, Germany, Greece, Georgia, Turkey, Iran, Sudan, Azerbaijan, Tajikistan, Uzbekistan. Kazakhstan is one of the world's major producers of coal, gas, ferrous and non-ferrous metals, corn, and products of stock breeding. More importantly, Kazakhstan is number one uranium producer in the world since 2009. Kazakhstan has been an important source of uranium for more than fifty years and is expected to play a dominant role in uranium production for the foreseeable future. Our country is a party to the Nuclear Non-Proliferation Treaty (NPT) as a non-nuclear-weapons state. Some 1300 nuclear warheads were destroyed after independence.

It has no nuclear power stations of its own and doesn't use any uranium byproducts.

Just a month ago, Kazakhstan was selected to host EXPO-2017 "Energy for the Future" Exhibition competing with Liege, Belgium. Living at that time already in Brussels, we were especially excited for our country. We have been receiving many calls and inquiries about this nomination. Foreigners were sincerely glad and at the same time surprised that Kazakhstan did so well. "So much has to be done to successfully host the exhibition!" they say in Kazakhstan, aware of the great responsibility involved. Now more people know about and support our country thanks to our nomination, and our job is to honor that support.

Once, while flying from Holland to Switzerland on KLM airlines, I was reading an article "Who are the Dutch?" in an inflight magazine: "From above, the Netherlands looks immaculate... Every square metre has a purpose, and the same order is reflected in society. A deal is a deal, four o'clock is four o'clock. A visit to family or friends is planned, and joining them for dinner only acceptable if it has been agreed in advance. 'Just be normal, that's crazy enough', goes the Dutch saying. It typifies the national character, which is termed 'Calvinistic'. Excessive behaviour is not appreciated in principle. Dutch leaders live in modest homes... Money-grabbing at the top is a mortal sin. Although the Netherlands is a constitutional monarchy, it has little regard for superiority.... Tulips, clogs, windmills, cheese and tolerance. That stereotype does well abroad".

This stereotype characterizes a small country of fifteen million people. Even if I wanted to stereotype our country, I could not. Kazakhstan has almost the same population size as Holland though it is a huge country, the ninth largest in the world, with the territory of 2,700,000 square kilometers spanning three time zones. And the population has striking regional differences.

Nowadays there is a huge mass of information available on Kazakhstan. But on the world scene, we still have to explain who we are, what our language is, what religion we confess. In short, the definitions are the following: the word "Kazakh" is derived from an ancient Turkic word meaning "independent, freemen". It reflects the Kazakh people's nomadic horseback culture.

The Kazakh language comes from the Turkic family of languages. Kazakh was written first during the 1860s with the Arabic script. Latin script was introduced later in 1929. In 1940 the Latin alphabet was in turn replaced by the Cyrillic alphabet, which was imposed for ideological reasons. However, recent plans have been made as part of a government modernization program in which the idea is to replace the Cyrillic alphabet with the Latin alphabet. No decision has yet been made due to a lengthy investigation into the consequences and costs of implementing this. One of the reasons for the switch to Latin is linked to the representation of the sounds of the Kazakh language which are not properly represented and this leads to difficulties with correct pronunciation.

Kazakh is an agglutinative, verb-final language with a subject-object-verb word order. With nine phonemic vowels, of which three are diphthongs, the language has vowel harmony, meaning that a soft vowel in the last syllable of a word requires the usage of a soft vowel in the affix. The same happens with the hard vowels. The result is a mellifluous flow of vowels and consonants. Kazakhstan is a mostly Muslim nation with an open- minded attitude toward religion. Most Kazakhs are Sunni Muslims. All religions of Kazakhstan (Muslims, Christian Orthodox, Catholics, Protestants, Buddhists, and Jews) are treated equally. It is a country where different faiths, ethnic backgrounds and cultures co-exist peacefully. "Kazakhstan has proven that a mostly Muslim nation does not have to be at odds –nor at war– with the rest of the world. Kazakhstan has demonstrated that Islam can be just as any other religion, at peace with itself and at peace with the world."[4] I enjoy telling people about my country. Lucky for me, it is my job as a wife of an ambassador; it is what I am supposed to do during lunches and dinners, at receptions, meetings, conferences, presentations, and personal contacts. Previously, I had a daily planner with a small map inside and I showed it to everyone who asked me where my country was, but that was ten or fifteen years ago. Today there is no lack of information thanks to Internet: whatever you want to know about Kazakhstan is just a click away. For a first-time visitor, for one who has never even heard of Kazakhstan, or for one who has never even seen it on the world map, try http://en.wikipedia.org/wiki/Kazakhstan. For more serious research, refer to US Central Intelligence Agency's website, which is listed in the top of the Google search engine for Kazakhstan (https://www.cia.gov/ library/publications/the-world-factbook/geos.kz.html). I want to stress that Americans tend to be consistent and precise in the way they present the data and facts; in a very simple and easily understood matter the data here is presented with the help of maps, pictures, statistics, all easily comprehensible and updated.

Sometimes people may resist learning more about other countries simply because some country names might sound hard to pronounce. This is a kind of linguistic stereotype, that the languages of exotic places are impossible to learn or understand. In fact, these words can often be

----

[4] P.23. Islam Without a Veil. Kazakhstan's Path of Moderation by Claude Salhani.

easily understood. For instance, the suffix -*stan* is found in many cities and countries' names, like Kazakhstan, Kyrgyzstan, Pakistan, Afghanistan, Turkmenistan, Uzbekistan, Tajikistan, Tatarstan, Kurdistan. The old name of India was Hindustan. *Stan* means *the place of*, or, *where one stand*s. Thus, *Kazakhstan* means *Land of the Kazakh*s. My name *Gulistan* is very well pronounced by foreigners, and this is surprising because it is long; *Gul* means *flower* and it signifies a flower *garden* (a garden being a place for plants).

Regarding unwelcome stereotypes, I remember one episode in Malta. As ambassador of Kazakhstan to the Italian Republic, my husband was also accredited to San Marino, Greece, and Malta. Later, due to the strengthening of the relationship between our country and Greece, a new embassy was set up. We were invited for the reception in Malta to celebrate the New Year. There were several ambassadors with their wives from the Congo, Pakistan, and the Philippines at our round table headed by the Ministry of Foreign Affairs' representative of Malta. When he found out that one of the ambassadors was from the Philippines, he exclaimed: "Oh, when I worked at our embassy in London, our house cleaner was Philippine!" The ambassador of the Philippines kept silent and so did the rest of us.

We all care about the well-being and the progress of our country, and we are proud to see our flag raised, when it means that we are able to help other countries. In 2010, the year after the earthquake in the region of Abruzzo, a hundred kilometers away from Rome, I happened to visit

Aquila, the city most damaged in the area. The trip to Aquila was organized by the "Insieme a Roma" ("Together in Rome") association supported by the Ministry of Foreign Affairs of Italy. I had never been in Aquila before but what I saw after the earthquake shocked me deeply. The historical centre of the city had been severely damaged. All the roads to the city were closed by the latticed gates and guarded by *carabinieri* (Italian policemen). There were hundreds of keys hung at the gates with the notes such as: "We hope to come back," "We don't have anything left," "Aquila will survive," "It is our home." In the very centre of town, a monument to the victims of the earthquake had been erected, covered by fresh flowers.

I knew that our government has contributed substantial resources to the reconstruction of the Church San Biagio di Amiternum and Oratory di San Giuseppe del Minimi (17th-18th century). The church was one of the most significant architectural constructions of baroque style in Aquila. When Italians found out that Kazakhstan paid for the reconstruction of the church, they applauded me as a representative of our country. I was on the verge of tears and I was definitely proud of my country! We went to see the church. The architect of the city came up to greet me. He told us about what had to be done to reconstruct what was left. Constant rain threatened further destruction of the city. It was being rebuilt but the reconstruction was proceeding slowly. Later, in *Libero*, an Italian daily newspaper, I read the article entitled *"L'Aquila mette in more Obama: 'Paga'. Il Kazakistan di Borat ha donato 1.700.000 euro. Il Governo USA ancora nulla. E Frattini manda il sollecito:*

'*Una figuraccia, specie se confrontata con il comportamento del piccolo Kazakistan., il quale ha dato 1,7 millioni di euro per la chiesa di San Biagio di Amiternum e per l'oratorio de San Giuseppe dei Minimi*"'This translates as: "The situation with Aquila faults Obama: 'Pay'. Kazakhstan of Borat has donated 1,700,000 euros. The US government has not paid anything yet. And Mr. Frattini reminds us: 'Poor numbers if particularly compared with what little Kazakhstan has done, which gave 1.7 million euros for reconstruction of the church of San Biagio di Amiternum and for the oratory of San Giuseppe of Minimi.'"

"Il Kazakistan di Borat" (Kazakhstan of *Borat*). This name deserves a bit of explanation because it has created a lot of confusion with the coming to cinema screens of a 2006 Hollywood comedy called *Borat: Cultural Learnings of America for Make Benefit Glorious Nation of Kazakhstan*. Exactly why Sacha Baron Cohen (Borat) — an English stand-up comedian, writer, actor, and voice actor — chose Kazakhstan as his place of origin is not clear and has never been understood by the audience, but the film has no connection whatsoever with Kazakhstan. Borat's Kazakhstan bears no resemblance to the real Kazakhstan. He definitely gets everything wrong about our country. The movie has become famous because Borat is offensive in the funniest ways and is simply disgusting! Ironically though, the government of Kazakhstan has officially thanked Sacha Baron Cohen for unintentionally promoting tourism in Kazakhstan.

There is a newly discovered sense of pride in Kazakhstan based on the idea of harmony, stability, and co-existence of various nationalities, ethnicities, and religious practices all living under one roof, and this is what makes devotion to one's country even stronger. If my daughters appear to be less attached to their own country than their parents are, it may in part be because two of them live abroad with their foreign husbands. When our family first moved abroad, the girls were still quite young and much more quickly adapted to the new places in a way becoming emotionally attached to every country where we have lived, so that their allegiance is in a way diffused. As for us adults, while we too have become somewhat affectionate for the countries where we have lived, we have always been aware of the fact that we have been on official missions in all these countries to represent our own.

Once I was on the airplane heading to Amsterdam and I saw a group of young Kazakhstan sportsmen enter the airplane, recalls one of our daughters, and they were all wearing blue and gold uniforms with the flag emblem on the front. At that moment I felt very proud. Especially to see young men and women going abroad to represent our country competing in the world of sports.

On the other hand, having lived abroad for a long period of time, in the USA, Great Britain, Spain, Italy, now Belgium, I feel attached to these countries and, when watching TV, listening to the news, or talking to somebody blaming or making bad remarks about one of these countries, I feel myself hurt as if they had talked badly about my own country. And not only I but my family also feels the same way.

In one striking example, the Italian President Giorgio Napolitano cancelled a planned dinner meeting with Peer Steinbruek in Berlin, February 27, 2013 after the German opposition chancellor candidate insulted two leaders from Italy's February 24-25 election. The Social Demo- crat, scheduled to take on Chancellor Angela Merkel in Germany's national election in September, was referring to Beppe Grillo, a former professional comedian, and ex-Prime Minister Silvio Berlusconi, whose alleged sexual exploits are well documented in the press. Steinbruek said: "To a certain extent, I'm appalled that two clowns have won. One professional clown who is also not offended if you call him one, Grillo, and another who is clearly a clown with a testosterone boost". In a response, the president of Italy, Napolitano, was highly offended by these comments. All major newspapers in Italy that day focused on these *"insulti tedeschi"* (German insults). The President of Italy was quoted as saying: *"Rispetto per Germania ma esigiamo rispetto!"* (We respect Germany but we demand respect for ourselves!) Even Maria, our daughter's mother-in-law was offended. She said: "We Italians criticize our government, our "clowns" a lot, but when our European partners, such as Germans, criticize us, we get very offended, because it is our domestic problem and Germans have no idea how complicated Italian politics work in the first place. I can only say, that it hurts our family, too."

It hurts also to hear negative comments about Russia, our neighboring country. The two nations share the world's longest land border. Kazakhstan and Russia have worked together after the collapse of the Soviet Union on their interstate issues with the national interests of each nation in mind. We have maintained our economic, cultural, scientific, and military cooperation. We are partners. We have a common history, culture, and language. My first school friend was Russian, and I still have lots of Russian friends, some of whom have left for Russia while some have remained in Kazakhstan. We have never had any problem socializing because of language or nationality. We are just friends. When I visit my friends in Moscow or talk to unknown Russian people, I feel this friendliness and respect of Russians towards Kazakhs. We have the same feelings towards Russians in Kazakhstan. Russia is a great nation with a great future. Once in Spain, my friend Geraldine Jones, wife of ambassador of Australia to Spain, asked me to help her to host the ladies. I was supposed to register guests by asking their names and the country they were from. The first lady told me she was from Slovakia, her husband was German, they came from Switzerland and their previous posting was Austria. Then she added: "I don't really know who we are as a family, we are so international, and that's why we can choose between any of these countries". When I had to go to Switzerland from Belgium in a car for the first time, I had to pass through Luxembourg, France, and Germany. I was expecting to see some kind of a border though I knew there was no actual border between these countries. Now Europe seems like one big country, which is astonishing. No boundaries, no border customs, no policemen.

Increasingly much is being written on the issue of foreignness, and how it should not be discriminated against and even more is being written to put the issue of foreignness on par with the historical struggles for abolition of slavery, racism, and discrimination against women. Some human-rights defenders argue that thinking of people as being "foreigners" is wrong and outdated.

The term "abolition of foreignness" signifies a quest to overcome discrimination and exclusion on the grounds of foreignness. The term "foreignness", according to a standard dictionary, denotes "the quality or state of being from, characteristic of or related to another country, area, people, etc.". It is a recent idea that foreign citizens have a human right to be treated as national citizens without discrimination. This idea, still philosophical, might seem vague, like the idea of a united Europe might have seemed until just a few decades ago. But it is a reality now: the European Union, "united in diversity". Half a century of European integration has shown that the European Union as a whole is greater than the sum of its parts. This modern tendency was nevertheless a vision of Socrates over 2000 years ago, when he said: "I am not an Athenian or a Greek, I am a citizen of the world." This might be thought of as moving the feeling of patriotism from the local to the world level. In human terms, there are tremendous gains in acting together and speaking with a single voice, as reflected in the song "United":

"I want to see the world united and learn to live as one We have to bring the world together/ we shall overcome".

Everyone should be entitled to a sense of belonging.

CHAPTER IX
VEILS AND FAIRYTALES

"When there is love in a marriage, there is harmony in the home; when there is harmony in the home, there is contentment in the community; when there is contentment in the community, there is prosperity in the nation; when there is prosperity in the nation, there is peace in the world."

Chinese proverb

When you live in a different country, a chance to attend a foreign wedding is a great experience to learn more about the culture. The memorable royal gathering at which we had the honor of attending was the wedding of Prince Felipe of Asturias to Letizia Ortiz Rocasolano of Spain on May 22nd 2004. Millions of people around the world watched the ceremony on television, making it Europe's biggest royal wedding in the last 23 years, since the wedding of Prince Charles and Diana Spencer. The wedding took place in the Cathedral Santa Maria la Real de la Almudena in Madrid. It had been nearly a century since the capital celebrated a royal wedding, as previous royal marriages took place in other cities of Spain and abroad. Over 1,400 guests gathered in the cathedral for the royal wedding. Among the many guests were members of 30 royal houses and 15 presidents and heads of states, including our president. King Juan Carlos and our president have a warm relationship and the King has visited our country several times.

All the talk in Spain was about the upcoming wedding. Everything from the dress of the bride to the guests of the royal wedding was discussed in details in newspapers, magazines, in the streets, bars, and restaurants. When we got the invitation, we found that the dress code for the wedding was a cocktail or national dress. Women of the diplomatic corps were sure we had to wear hats though it was not indicated in the invitation. I hate hats! I hate them because they ruin my hairstyle and because they don't suit me, I look like a mushroom. And I regretted I didn't have a nice national dress, and later I regretted it for the second time when I watched cameramen taking photos of people mainly in national suits. If I had had a national dress, I wouldn't have needed to wear a hat. So, I had to look for a hat to match my dress with a very specific color –a kind of violet. It would be easier in my case to find a dress than a hat. I still have it and I hope I never use it again. I didn't put it on my head on the wedding day, I just left it in the bus for the diplomatic corps. Besides, I noticed that the dress code was not strictly followed, sometimes even disregarded. Formality is gradually giving way to the informality in a changing internationalizing world. But I had learned to follow the rules of protocol.

Unfortunately, we learn most things on the spot: how to shake hands wearing elbow-length gloves, how to bow and make curtsies, how to greet royalty, how to express gratitude or condolences, what titles to use when addressing people, and so on and so forth. And I noticed also that some diplomats don't follow the rules of protocol when greeting the Royal family: women don't curtsy and men don't bow their heads. In Spain, bows and curtsies are done on a regular basis, as even their children greet Their Majesties with a bow or curtsy. There is no precedent for men to curtsy but once I saw a man become confused and instead of bowing he made a curtsy.

In London in 1996, we attended a royal reception at the Buckingham Palace. The dress code was an evening gown, which I found at the store in our neighborhood. When a shop-assistant learned that I was going to go to the palace, she said: "Unfortunately, we don't have this opportunity". It is true, we as foreigners and diplomats have the opportunity to visit places which citizens of the country don't visit; we meet kings and queens, princes and princesses, famous people, and visit rare sites and places of special interest.

Each embassy got three invitations for the reception: chargé d'affaires, minister-counselor, and counselor. The dress code was stated in the invitation: black tie (ladies should wear a long dress). Three women from our embassy were in search of an appropriate dress. I bought a black sleeveless dress, long black gloves, and a shawl with feathers to cover my shoulders. It was my first long dress. My lady friend whose husband was minister- counselor of our embassy bought a long black dress with sleeves. The third woman kept her dress secret until the day before the reception. It was like a bolt lightning from a clear sky when we heard from her that wearing black was not suitable (black is appropriate when the Court is mourning) and she was going to wear an emerald green dress with jewelry which she had rented beforehand. It sounds funny now but at that moment we felt like dying if we couldn't find a dress of another color. Our husbands unwillingly followed us to different stores but were willing to pay whatever money necessary to see the end of the race. My lady friend and I burst into laughter when we ran into each other in one of the London stores! We hadn't found anything suitable after all.

When we entered the palace, it was a relief to see many women in black. Practically every woman dressed in black. Besides, foreigners are always excused for not following the rules of the country. The invitation for the royal palace didn't say anything about the color of a dress, so it was not an issue after all. The atmosphere of the reception, ladies in beautiful long dresses, the orchestra, the ball — everything looked like a fairytale, which I didn't want to come to an end. We were introduced to the Queen, Duke of Edinburgh, and Prince Charles, who had just come back from an official visit from Kazakhstan. "The Queen hadn't changed at all, elegant as always", I thought.

I still keep my black long dress as a reminder of that fairytale evening and thanked myself for not renting it.

Those elegant, long dresses are rarely worn nowadays. The last time I wore it was when we were invited to the New Year reception at the Royal Palace in Spain. All diplomatic receptions in Spain were elegant, I have to say.

In Spain, on different occasions, I learned to wear colorful Spanish shawls and fans. The Spanish shawl, the *mantón*, is one of the country's landmark garments. A classic Spanish shawl is the type worn by flamenco dancers. If it is made with white or beige lace, it can be used as a wedding veil, mantilla, often worn on the head, frequently elevated by high curved combs. I bought a *mantilla* for my daughter's wedding in Kazakhstan. Spanish shawls are the ideal accessory. Solids and prints add color to a neutral or black outfit. They also add warmth, and they can liven up jeans and a t-shirt, adding gypsy allure. They are long-lasting wardrobe enhancers, and they also travel well. I know Spanish women who keep them in their families as heirlooms, wearing them occasionally and taking good care of them. They are often hand-embroidered by grandmothers or great-grandmothers. The fan, *abanico*, has always been ubiquitous in Spain and not just for the heat. During the first months in Spain, we were invited to the Russian opera in Madrid. Our seats were in the first row. In a while, I heard a kind of rustling. I turned my head and I saw hundreds of fans which looked like butterflies flapping their beautiful wings. Fans became not just a practical item, to keep cool oneself or whisk away insects, but an object of beauty with distinctive meanings. The fan is also still used as a code of communication between lovers. Moving fast and short sweeps over the chest means *I am not available*; opening the fan and touching her cheek means *I like you*; hitting her right hand with her fan means *I don't like you*; carrying the fan closed and hanging in her right hand means *I am engaged*; and so on. I also keep Spanish fans and use them frequently, bearing in mind the image of my friend, Marisa Torres as a typical beautiful Spanish *doña*. The precious fan I have is the gift of *Damas Diplomáticas* for my job as the vice- president of the association.

The first time my husband presented credentials to a head of state was to the King of Spain in 1999. At the agreed time, Almaz was escorted from our residence in Madrid by the Deputy Chief of Protocol in the official ceremonial car, flying the Kazakhstan flag and preceded by a motorcade to the Ministry of Foreign Affairs of Spain.

He was greeted with a salute and afterwards accompanied by a protocol representative on his way to the Palacio Real (Royal Palace) in a carriage drawn by six horses. Upon the arrival to the palace the Royal Guard honored the new ambassador. After the ceremonial introduction, Almaz handed his credentials to the King of Spain Juan Carlos I, followed by the traditional private audience with the King. In Spain, a spouse doesn't accompany her husband to present credentials inside the palace but is allowed to stay at the palace entrance. Just before leaving Spain after six years living there, we had a private audience with the King. We didn't feel pressured speaking to His Majesty. He invited us to come back again at another posting.

When we presented our credentials in Malta, a horse carriage picked us up from the hotel where we stayed and we crossed the main square to reach the presidential palace. I had to wear a hat again and a suit for that occasion. In San Marino my husband presented credentials to the Captains Regent. In a suit without a hat or gloves, I also accompanied my husband. In Greece, I was not allowed to be present when my husband handed over the credentials. We visited this country many times on different occasions, official and unofficial, and lived in the same hotel, which served as our residence address. In Italy, credentials are handed over to the President by ambassadors only, as no spouse is allowed to accompany her husband. Wives of ambassadors are invited only once a year in Italy. It looks as though the dress code does not exist at all in Italy as you can see women in cocktail and long dresses at the same time. In Belgium, my husband presented the credentials to the King of Belgium in a group of other ambassadors and had a group talk afterwards. Spouses were not allowed to accompany their husbands. We greeted the King, the Queen, the Princess, and Prince at the Royal reception in January, 2013. *Palais Royal* is the official palace of the Belgian monarchy. It is one of the most beautiful buildings in Brussels. The reception was held in the *Mirror Room*, a creation of Jan Fabre. The ceiling and the central chandelier were covered with the wing cases of 1.4 million Thai jewel beetles, which reflect the light with a curiously vibrant energy. The unusual emerald green color of the ceiling stood out against light outside. The dress code was a cocktail or national dress though the reception was organized to celebrate the New Year.

On the March 13th, 2013 Almaz presented his credentials to His Royal Highness (HRH) the Grand Duke of Luxembourg. According to protocol, ladies were to wear a long afternoon gown, a hat, and gloves (the length and color to fit with the dress) or a national costume. A dress code for the Head of Mission is either a long black tailcoat with a white waistcoat and decoration (no gloves) or a national costume. I accompanied my husband, together with three members of the embassy. The male members followed the dress code of the male ambassador and the female members followed the dress code of the female ambassador or wife of the ambassador. I chose to wear a national dress, and so did our woman diplomat. My husband looked impressive with his decorations. Among several Kazakhstan government awards, there were decorations from the government of Spain and Italy. He put them on for the first time all together.

In Luxembourg, we stayed at the hotel Le Royal.

At 3:00 p.m. an aide-de-camp called on us at the hotel to take us to the Royal Palace in a car (old Rolls-Royce) provided by the Court. The day was sunny! The previous day we had been heading to Luxembourg in a car taking a slippery highway, met a traffic jam, and had a few stops. It had been snowing and was cold.

We were escorted by police cars to the palace. Our car was comfortable enough for five people: a driver, an aide-de-camp (a tall military man), another military man in the same uniform in front, and us seated in the back.

Diplomats from our embassy were following us in another car. On the way to the palace, people in the street were waving at the procession and taking pictures. When we reached the palace, the palace guard saluted us. In the main hall, we were greeted by a Chamberlain of the Grand Duke and a Lady in Waiting. Then we proceeded to the first floor in the following order: Almaz as the Head of Mission and the Chamberlain on his left; I followed with the Lady in Waiting on my left; and our diplomats accompanied by the aide-de-camp followed us. In the hall on the first floor, we were received by the Marshall of the Court. It was my husband's duty to introduce me and his staff to the Marshall. Then the Marshall of the Court took my husband alone into the audience room, called the King's Room, where he introduced Almaz to His Highness the Grand Duke. I was waiting in the Yellow Room of the Palace together with the Lady in Waiting. Our diplomats remained in the hall together with the members of the suite of HRH. I couldn't help admiring the rooms of the Palace and asking the Lady a few questions about tapestries and pictures of the Yellow Room in particular. She was polite but not talkative at all.

It might have been boring for her to respond to the same questions as usually several heads of missions hand credentials to HRH the same day. Imagine if all spouses were curious like me.

After having greeted His Royal Highness by bowing, Almaz submitted his Letters of Credence to the Grand Duke at the presence of the Marshall of the Court and pronounced a few words of introduction. I couldn't watch the ceremony this time as I was in another room but I remember how it was usually done when I accompanied my husband in Malta where he handed credentials to the President of Malta in my presence. When the door of the audience room was opened, I entered the room and the Marshall of the Court introduced me to His Royal Highness. I made a curtsy. Then HRH invited us to the Ball Room where a photo was taken. HRH was standing between us, me on the left and Almaz on the right.

After taking photos, we proceeded to the King's Room where we had a private audience with HRH. It was a comfortable room with a functioning fireplace. The Grand Duke was seated on the sofa and we took our seats in front of HRH. The Grand Duke started the conversation by making a comparison between the size of Luxembourg and Kazakhstan. He said: "Kazakhstan is a bit bigger than Luxembourg". Later he impressed us by knowing how big the territory of our country was. He made detailed questions and remarked on almost everything, even about the fate of the Aral Sea. (The name of the sea was very often associated with the word "problem". The world's fourth largest freshwater lake was 90% dried up. Now, with an $85 million engineering project, and collaboration between the World Bank and Kazakhstan government, the doomed sea is coming back to life).

I didn't even notice that fifteen minutes of the audience with HRH had come to an end. According to protocol, the Marshall of the Court opened the door and let our diplomats enter the King's Room and they were introduced to HRH by my husband in their order of precedence. When

HRH had taken leave, we all left the room in the order in which we entered, slightly bowing our heads to the direction of HRH. Then the Chamberlain, the Lady in Waiting, and the aide-de-camp led us to the ground floor, where we all signed the Golden Book of the Palace in a small room with just one table and two medium-sized tapestries on the walls. In the hall, we had to wait a bit for the car to come and the aide-de-camp told us that there were not enough people to perform the ceremony. Then, we were taken to the hotel in the cars in which we had come, taking the same places in them.

It was a big relief, as it was stressful because of the responsibility each of us felt. Every step was taken strictly according to protocol. Young diplomats of our mission put on their long black tailcoats for the first time in their lives, bowing to the Grand Duke, having a conversation with Chamberlain and other people of the court. It was a fairytale with the guard and the royal ceremonies that none of us would ever forget.

It was even more memorable as on the same day, March 13th, my lucky number (I was born on the 13th of August, my daughter and my mom were also born on the 13th of January and April, respectively), the 266th pontiff of the Roman Catholic Church, the first non- European leader of the church in more than 1,000 years, the cardinal from Argentina, Jorge Mario Bergoglio was elected with a puff of white smoke from the chimney of the Sistine Chapel.

I attended many international weddings while being abroad: American, Russian, Italian, Arab, Spanish, French, Austrian. Each wedding is a reflection of country's culture and is interesting to observe from the point of view of a foreigner. I had a chance to be invited by my dearest friends to attend their daughters or sons' weddings not only as a guest but as a close friend. My friend, Princess Nur, invited me to the marriage of her son in Spain and her daughter in Jordan, and I attended both weddings. Also, I was invited to a beautiful wedding ceremony in France by my friend Marie-Dominique; Marisa Torres invited me to the wedding of her son in Spain; and I had the pleasure of attending the wedding of Martha Lucifero's daughter in Italy. I had fun in addition to having the pleasure of being able to support my friends, of being close to their families, and of having wonderful memories of the events. It evokes what the famous Russian writer Leo Tolstoy said: "All happy families are alike…" I wish them happiness!

Attending weddings, I also made comparisons with our Kazakh weddings, which vary from region to region, from countryside to city, from common people to the *nouveau riche*. In our ancient history, weddings lasted for weeks, brides were kidnapped by grooms. In olden times, there were mostly non-consensual bride kidnappings when the bride and groom didn't know each other or the groom didn't have money to pay the bride's family or the bride declined the groom's proposal. Nowadays consensual bride kidnapping takes place in southern regions of Kazakhstan and it is considered to be a harmless and fun tradition. In a typical case, the bride verbally consents to marriage one day and then her boyfriend later surprises her by "kidnapping" her.

In Kazakhstan, marriages tend to take on the Western style, though Kazakh customs and traditions are also followed. Marriage in Kazakhstan is a union of two families, as in Italy or other countries. Kazakhs interpret the word "family member" very broadly. All descendants of one grandfather up to the seventh generation are regarded as close relatives. That is why the ancient custom requires knowing one's ancestors and prohibits the marriage within one and the same bloodline.

In-laws in Kazakhstan become immediate family after the marriage of their children. The two fathers-in- law find many ways to start their friendship by going fishing, hunting, doing business, and so forth while the mothers-in-law do the same by going shopping, taking turns caring for the babies, etc.. From then on, the in- laws go on vacation and visit friends together. There is no stronger bond than theirs. When you find similarities between cultures in these basic human ways, you get a sense of closeness to the host country; you feel you are at home.

With regard to marriage, weddings in Kazakhstan are worth describing in general. Kazakh weddings are the spectacular and, at the same time, complicated. Time passes, governments change, new generations replace older ones, but the Kazakh weddings have remained almost the same, with some variations, depending on the region and status.

When young people decide to marry, the parents first meet to introduce themselves to each other. The future bride is presented with golden earrings as a sign of blessing given by a groom's mother. Then a series of visits starts: families introduce their relatives, giving priority to the older generation. They have to give their blessings in turn. Aunts and uncles also actively participate in the family reunion. Gift exchanges accompany each gathering. Each Kazakh family has lots of presents in stock for all sizes and both genders. You might even get something you presented once to somebody else. This happens because Kazakhs love being invited and receiving guests at their homes.

When the date of the wedding is fixed, both families compete to host the best wedding ceremony. It is a challenge for both to do their own wedding. In fact, there are two weddings: the first is put on by the bride's family, the other by the groom's family. The guests are almost the same; they just move from one wedding to another. When the bride moves out from the parents' house, there is another ceremony. Women get together in the place where the bride will live and aunts of the bride display the bride's belongings: furniture, dishes, clothes–a dowry given by the bride's mother. This is followed by the exchange of money on seeing the bride's dowry from the side of a groom. The demonstration of the bride's dowry is appreciation of the bride's family well-being, the bride's mother's efforts to do her best in raising her daughter. It is usually accompanied by blessings on the part of a senior among the guests. Traditionally, there is a great number of presents during a matchmaking when both sides invite each other back and forth.

Kazakhs are very fond of responding to the joy of another. You can get money or a gift on the spot for announcing good news, like a newborn baby, or even for opening a bride's veil because it is considered to be an honor, for cutting the baby's nails for the first time (which is also a privilege), for receiving a diploma, a document, or even a driving license, etc.. It is our tradition to share the joy of achievements small or large.

Then comes the actual wedding. There is always a party organizer, a toastmaster, called the *tamada*, who is found among actors. His job (usually it is a man) is to entertain people during the wedding by proposing toasts to the guests, telling funny stories, and singing. He has the right to introduce other people to make a toast –no refusal accepted and one should ask his permission to make a toast.

When my nephew was going to marry, we were looking for a *tamada*. We were horrified when we first saw him: tall, tight pants, a big ring with a skull on it on his finger, a black hat. My sister hesitated at first. But as there was no time to look for another *tamada*, she finally accepted his offer. We didn't have time to see his script, and we didn't talk about the sequence of toasts, which is very important in our country. Hierarchy is respected in Kazakhstan. The senior in attendance makes the first toast. Usually, the scenario of the wedding is discussed between a toastmaster and a host. Our *tamada* appeared in the same outfit on the wedding day, quickly changed his clothes and asked for a list of toasts. That's all! It seemed for us he was improvising as we hadn't discussed anything beforehand. He was running around, paying attention to everyone, joking, singing, dancing. He actually didn't have a break for six hours! He played a leading role in our "performance". I think the spontaneous scenario directed by him made the wedding sparkle. When the party was over, everybody was asking for his business card. I have never seen a funnier, more energetic, harder-working *tamada* than him.

As for the toasts, Kazakhs are considered to be orators. Every Kazakh is a singer, and almost every toast is followed by a song. By the way, the more extended and the more eloquent a toast, the louder the applause will be. But some orations can have unexpected consequences. At the wedding of our daughter in Kazakhstan, my father-in-law was to make the first toast as the eldest from both families. His two sons (my husband was among them) requested that he not speak too long. He nodded his head and started his speech by saying: "I am a veteran of war and labor…". In fact, he had embarked on his life story. By the end of his speech, which lasted for forty minutes, he had forgotten the name of a bride, his own granddaughter.

There is a Kazakh anecdote about the toasts. A man is carrying a carpet (this being one of the popular gifts in Kazakhstan during the Soviet times). His neighbor asks him where he is going. He says he is invited to a wedding. After a while the neighbor sees him carrying the carpet back home. He asks him what happened, why he is carrying the carpet back. The man says he was not given a toast.

Kazakhs are inventive by nature and quickly absorb the latest trends in organizing weddings while keeping our beautiful traditions. I will always remember and exemplify the wedding of our youngest daughter, Asem. Her wedding was a melting pot of different people, cultures and languages. Having studied at ten schools over the span of twenty years, she made very good friends with people from all over the world. For her wedding on August 1st, 2009, about fifty of her friends flew in from several countries across the globe representing twenty-one nationalities: Swiss, German, Swedish, Peruvian, Spanish, Colombian, Japanese, Russian, Italian, American, Argentinean, Kazakh, Liechtensteinian, Somalian, Norwegian, British, French, Sri Lankan, Canadian, Cuban, Mexican. The wedding felt less like a wedding and more like a fun reunion and a big party where all the young people were celebrating just being together. Asem had not seen many of these friends in years and here they all were sharing one of the most important days of her life with her, with their warm hugs, wishes, and presents and the sheer joy of being all together again. When one meets a good friend again it always feels like no time has passed. More surprising still was that they could all fly into Austria on such a short notice. Asem and Markus's engagement period was two months long!

Asem and Markus got married in the charming town of Feldkirch, Austria. The civil ceremony was short but very touching, followed by an aperò and finally dinner and dancing. It was mainly a European wedding but with a few elements of Kazakh tradition. Before the wedding, we had an occasion to meet Markus's parents and his sister. According to our tradition, we made a typical Kazakh present –*shapan* (a long colourful overcoat), which is one of the ancient outer-garments of Kazakh traditional clothes and Kazakh jewellery for women. A *shapan* is presented to guests as a sign of respect. And we were pleased to see Markus's parents wearing our *shapans* at the wedding. We also brought Kazakh souvenirs as *bonbonnière* for all the guests. Just for having fun, everybody was served vodka. Everything at the wedding was quite standard and simple, nothing lavish or posh, and it was the most beautiful wedding I have ever been to. The wedding was a real celebration and I believe it had much to do with the mix of cultures, the amount of young people, and the lack of traditional protocol.

The day after the wedding, we hosted a brunch to say thank you and goodbye to all those friends who had come from abroad to the wedding. At the end of the brunch, Annelies, Markus's mother, took Asem aside at the restaurant where we hosted the brunch and presented her with a beautiful sapphire and diamond bracelet, which she had inherited from her late father. I was very touched by the subtlety of this generous gesture. The family of my son-in-law was welcoming my daughter into their family with the precious gift and given in such a modest way, not making a big deal of it, just warmly saying "Welcome to our family". I was also surprised at this gesture because when a couple gets engaged in the Kazakh tradition, it is customary for the parents of the groom to give the bride a piece of jewellery, typically a pair of gold earrings. Before the wedding I gave my daughter the pearl earrings which I inherited from my father. It was a touching moment for all of us. The bond between two families strengthened right after this little ceremony. They got a daughter and we got a son.

In a short time there will be a wedding of our daughter in Italy. We are looking forward to meet Gian Marco's relatives, a big Italian friendly family, to have another son, to welcome our friends from Spain and Italy and other countries we worked and lived in and learned from. For us, for our world, the Chinese proverb has come true.

CHAPTER X
CHARITY BEGINS AT HOME

"It's not how much we give but how much love we put into giving."

Mother Teresa

When we were to move to Brussels, our grandchildren were seven and a half. We decided to give their toys, books, and clothes to a local charity. First of all, we asked them to keep the things they needed and put them in their own boxes, explaining to them that we could not take everything with us as we had baggage limits. The kids got upset — they were used to getting toys, not giving them away.

Once in their early childhood we read a story called the "Blue Train" by Gianni Rodari. It was about an orphan named Francesco who was dreaming of having a blue train from a toy store he was passing by. For the first time our grandkids discovered for themselves that there were poor children, with no parents to take care of them, no toys to play with. They were touched by the fate of an orphan. So, we had to remind them about Francesco, and we were greatly touched by their willingness to help the poor. After that incident, every time I asked them to sort their toys out, they would tell me: "Granny, you can take all our toys to orphans!" They had learned what it means to share.

When I first met Irene Koch in Spain, she brought me once to Colegio de Primaria y Infantil "San Pio X", the school that her severely disabled son Lucas attended. This school has several special-needs classes. When we went to the class to see the children, I met Carmen de Celis Estrada, the head of the school. When I became vice-president of the Association of Diplomatic Ladies of Asia and Australia in Madrid, I suggested establishing a charity fund for Lucas's school. Irene came to our meeting to give a talk on the school, the children, and their needs. Our first donation was nine hundred and forty-eight Euros and the school was able to rent a bus for travels. Later, we donated a Christmas tree, decorations, toys, candies, and small gifts, and I still keep a paper Christmas tree with all the handprints made by Lucas and his peers. That was how it all started.

Irene's youngest son, Lucas, has mitochondrial disease, a rare malady that debilitates the body's energy mechanism (the mitochondrion) and causes multiple severe disabilities. He cannot speak or walk and has the mental capacity of a baby. His elder brother, Jonas, on the other hand, is very active and capable. Last year, he finished his education at the European School of Alicante (Spain) and now is in Hamburg, Germany, studying in a hotel-management school. I have known these boys ever since Jonas was four and Lucas was two years old. Maybe the finest achievement of Irene and Thomas's child raising has been the strong brotherly bond between Jonas and Lucas. Jonas, whatever moment he has, takes care of his younger brother, and Lucas is happy to have his elder brother around him. In 2003, when John Paul II visited Spain, Lucas and Jonas were among those children who greeted the Pope. There was a section in the stadium especially reserved for people with disabilities. When the Pope asked what his dream was, Jonas, looking at Lucas, said that he dreamed of playing and talking with his younger brother.

When Irene moved to Alicante due to her husband's job, she became even more immersed in the problems of children with disabilities. After meeting other women who had kids with severe disabilities, such as Matilde Diaz, Paloma Arroyo, and Rosi Orive, they formed an association which is called AODI (The Association for Leisure for the Mentally Disabled of Alicante). This non-profit organization began with the aim of giving parents a small break, when volunteers take the children with disabilities to parks, farms and many other places of fun and excitement. Meanwhile the parents can breathe easily for a short time with the rest of the family, knowing that their children are in reliable hands, and afterwards they can return to their task of caretaking with new energy. At one of the AODI meetings, I was nominated an honorary member of the association. Receiving an official letter, I felt this nomination to be a great honor.

In 2009 a group of family and friends of Irene and Thomas established the Foundation which bears Lucas's name: Lucas Koch Foundation (known in Spanish as Fundación Lucas Koch, a.k.a. FLK). It implements projects to help children and adolescents suffering from multiple severe disabilities. This year in Alicante, Spain, FLK is starting to build a residence, inspired by a Dutch model, for seven children with disabilities. The residence is not only equipped inside for young people of great dependence, but it also will have a sensory garden (fragrances, colors, and textures), a therapeutic pool, and a therapy center. Approximately hundred families will be served yearly by the FLK Center.

Anne Marie Otten, the President of FLK, Erika Müller, First Vice-President, Irene Koch, former Second Vice-President, members Carmen Calvet, Karin Pascual, Elena Guembe, Esther Rivera, team and board members, as well as Honorary Board Trustee, Her Royal Highness Sharifa Nur Nasser Jamil Alaoun, are among the many people who are making the dreams come true for these children. I am proud to be part of this great team. There was the initiative of FLK to sell bricks for the construction of the residence for children with disabilities in order to raise money. Each brick has the name of the donor on it. Our embassy in Italy organized a charity event to collect money for the association. People from many different countries came to offer their support and make their contribution for Spanish children. This event displayed a unity of souls, a unity of countries, and the power of solidarity.

I always thought that charity is expression of caring and compassion for others. It is part of human nature to love and care, to support and give, to share one's joy and be generous. Winston Churchill once said: "What is the use of living, if it not be to strive for noble causes and to make this muddled world a better place for those who will live in it after we are gone?"

Once at school, Jonas was given a task to write about heroes and he chose his brother to be a hero:

I admire my brother Lucas. Everything I do, I do for him. I do not want to be like him finally, but he has not done a bad thing on purpose in his life. He seems to be at peace and I would love to know how that feels, even if it was just for a moment. My brother is not like the average person on earth, he is special and I know because I live with him and see what he does every day. Life has not been fair to him but even so, I wish that in some aspects I was more like him. For me, a hero is a person you respect, follow and admire. I have the feeling that people think my brother follows me but I actually follow him. I respect him and admire him for everything he has done, does and will do. He has changed my life completely and I have done efforts to adapt my way of living to the one of my hero, Lucas. Many people think that being a hero means that you have super powers, can fly and can run really fast. They are wrong. My brother is a hero for me and he is in a wheelchair. People have to evaluate the interior part of the person and then you can find more than just one hero in our daily life. Anyone can be a hero.

My nephew, Dimash, is also disabled. He is a son of my most beloved sister, Gulnara. I remember him since his first year, spent in hospitals month after month, and I recall my sister with her worries and despair, and constant crying. Her husband left her, not being able to face the challenges. He chose to marry another woman with no children right after the divorce. It took years for my sister to accept and adjust to the reality, to realize that life was going on, but she lost any hope of seeing improvements in her son's health. He is twenty-eight now. He is not in a wheel-chair; he walks, he talks like a four-year-old boy, he plays with toys, his hands are weak, and he is always supervised.

Dimash has an elder brother, Erkin, who, like Jonas, suffered for not being able to play or talk to his brother at least at the beginning when both were little. Now that he has his own family, his own son, he has become more patient towards his brother. As often happens, the more troubled the child, the more attention we give him. My sister had her hands full with her disabled son and left her elder son by himself. He needed her attention, too, but it took all her time and strength to spend on her little one, who was so helpless and so dependent. Thinking of my dearest sister and my dearest friend, I often ask myself: "Would I be able to cope with this challenge if I were in their shoes?" It would be the toughest of challenges, even for the imagination, and it is impossible to know the answer.

My sister joined an Association of Parents of Children with Disabilities of Almaty (ARDI) and got involved in various activities of the association. I met the president of the association, a mother of a child with disabilities, and I made a donation after the sale of my first book, and visited school's facilities. Like many associations working with children with disabilities, this association was established by a group of parents- supporters in 1991. It supports 400 families who are raising children with disabilities, providing medical rehabilitation, correctional support, and education for children and young people with special needs. Visiting the school facilities, I watched children with disabilities drawing and making crafts. It was amazing creativity they put into their works. I couldn't resist buying a few of those creations.

My nephew continues to attend a school for children with disabilities. He has been there for many years now with no chance of graduating. He makes friends at his school, he loves watching movies about soldiers and he loves spending time with his mother.

Since we left Kazakhstan nineteen years ago, I hardly saw him except rare encounters with him during my visits home. Recently our seven-year-old granddaughter saw him for the first time. We hadn't told her anything in advance, to let her make up her own mind, and during lunch she identified him as being different and she got confused. She did not say a word; she did not even ask us anything, possibly forming her own perception. When we came back home, we started a conversation with her explaining why he behaved in a strange way. We explained to her that some kids were born this way, that they did no harm, and that, moreover, they needed our constant care and understanding. The least we could do for them was not to isolate them, become more sensitive towards them, and try in any way we could to help those deprived of care.

A way to help children understand other differences, such as disability is provided in the words of advice of Arancha Martínez, social worker with the Lucas Koch Foundation:

Small children don't usually notice someone having a disability, unless it is very obvious. However, at an age of about four years, children begin to notice whether a person cannot walk or eat with the rest of the children, and they often ask indiscrete questions. The way to respond to these initial innocent and curious questions can affect the way in which your child approaches disability, and how he or she begins to treat and empathize with other persons and how that treatment and those feelings evolve as the child grows older.

The first time that you cross paths with someone who has a disability and your child notices, do not tell him or her not to look or to keep walking, because your child will think that the disabled person should be avoided and that no questions should be asked. Take the opportunity to have a conversation about the differences. Explain that we are all different in some way, such as the color of the hair or skin. To promote the attitude of acceptance and inclusion, adults should clarify the differences.

We should try to answer the questions of children directly and not give long complicated explanations. If they ask you why the man in the supermarket is in a wheelchair, we should explain he has a problem with his legs. The answers should be simple. If you don't know the answer to one of the questions our child asks, simply say that you don't know. It is better to focus on the person and not on the disability and not to refer to children that do not have a disability as "normal children", as this implies that the others are not normal. Children catch words immediately and store them in their memory and later it would be more difficult to persuade them not to use this or that word.

We should emphasize equalities: one child can have physical or mental disability but continues to be a child. We should indicate what they have in com- mon, such as age, height, or even the same favorite color.

Sometimes children are worried about a disability being "contagious" or "catching". It is vital to make it clear that this is not the case and that they can go up to disabled children and even play with them. And if a child speaks about a disability being "weird", tell the child that it is not nice to make fun of others and explain how much those words can hurt .1

To foment this sort of understanding , Irene worked up a unique project to be undertaken at schools, a program entitled "Welcome to My World". It is an idea of inviting children without disabilities to visit her world – the world of the disability. Irene's brother, David Nesbitt, who has collaborated with the Lucas Koch Foundation, describes the program:

It is a set of various activities designed for children without disabilities to feel what difficulties disabled children face in their everyday lives. In one activity, children would sit in wheelchairs and operate them to go through an obstacle course in order to have the sensation of not being able to walk. In another activity, children would be blindfolded, as in some games, such as pin the tail on the donkey, but they would be asked to use a cane and try to find their way around another small obstacle course to feel what it is not to be able to see. In yet another activity, they would wear headphones that would make hearing difficult and try to make out what other people say to them. To feel what the isolation of autism is like, they would be given a set of pictures and sit in a Plexiglas box and try to communicate with others.

The idea is to understand what others go through in that other world, a world which is as familiar to us and as foreign to us as the moon. We all know about the moon, but not very much, and we've never been there. It would be fascinating to go, but maybe not a place we would like to stay very long, because it would soon become clear what a difficult place it is to live.

In fact, a sensation I had seeing disabled children wearing padded garments, was that they were wearing a space suit, and being in the wheelchair is like using one of those little machines that astronauts use to move around in outer space. With that, the project took on a sense of exploration and adventure. The learning adventure of going to the moon.

So, the invitation to this other world is meant to be an educational way for children without disability to come closer to disabled children and learn that, regardless of our abilities, we can all be together and share our world, rather than relegating the disabled to a cold, dark, distant place where we never want to go.

To give the child more the sense of travelling and exploring, a passport was designed to enter that world, with four visas to visit different realms: physical, visual, auditory, and mental disability. The ultimate aim is for a child without disability to feel familiar with and comfortable in that other world. For a child, this is a way of making the other world and our world one. For an adult, it is social integration. That would mean the end of isolation for one of the most defenseless sectors of society. For me, it is a return ticket to this world for my sister.

The project has been implemented in the European School Alicante (Spain) and several public schools. Kids have had a great time and have learned a lot. They have had a memorable experience. One of the students responded to the teachers' question "Are you having fun?" in the following way: "Teacher, this is not to have fun; the important thing is to learn". Another four-year- old boy said to his father, who was going to park his car in a place for disabled people: "If you want to take the parking place you should also take the disability".

The educational community, both the teachers as well as the directors, consider these activities to be necessary and appropriate. They consider the project to have contributed enormously to the personal development of the students, who now are more prepared to understand the physical and mental differences and to adopt a more understanding and integrating attitude towards possible situations of social exclusion.

With this project, Irene came to Brussels, where I was living, to take part in the Eighth European Citizens Initiative "High-Quality European Education for All" at European Economic and Social Committee on December 6,

2012. The conference was organized by MEET European Education Trust presided by Ana Gorey. For four days at the European Parliament, European Commission, and European Economic and Social Committee, Irene and I were immersed in the discussions on disability issues, and common education problems.

In 2003 the European Parliament Disability Support Group was established with the backing of the Secretary- General and the Director-General for Personnel. It currently consists of about twenty officials from a variety of disability groups and operates on a voluntary basis. At one of the meetings a man with Down Syndrome took the floor and said: "Words create barriers and reinforce stereotypes. Help us to break stereotypes by using person-first language. Please, do not call me a Down Syndrome person. I am an adult with Down Syndrome.

I am a person first and foremost. I was just born with an extra chromosome."

We are really dealing with stereotypes more than diversity. There is no real understanding of the world of disability. There are thirty million disabled people in Europe. We do not even know what words should be used to name a person with disabilities. For instance, a blind person is called a person with a visual disability or visually impaired; a deaf person is called hearing impaired; a person with a physical disability is handicapped, disabled, invalid, lame, or deformed; a person with a mental disability is, mental retarded, deficient, intellectually challenged, a person with a learning difference; and person without a disability is simply referred to as a normal person and those with disability as "not normal".

On March 9th, 2013, I left for Alicante to take part in the conference on Raising Awareness on Disability and Social Inclusion, a big event initiated by my friend Irene, held under the auspices of the European School Alicante and the Office for Harmonization in the Internal Market (OHIM), in the context of the European Citizens' Initiative (ECI) during the Year of the European Citizen 2013 and attended by Vice-president of OHIM, Mayor of Alicante, the Council Advisor for Social Wellbeing of the Regional Government of Valencia (Generalitat Valenciana), Secretary General of the European Schools, President of MEET European Education Trust, Directors of European Schools. I learned a great deal from Irene and Arancha, who explained many aspects of disability: terminology, types, wrong attitudes, and personal experience.

During the conference, we had an opportunity to take part in different workshops of the program "Welcome to My World" on physical, visual, auditory, and mental disability. With passports to "My World" (the world of disability) we put ourselves in the shoes of those who live with disability. Seated in a wheelchair I could hardly move. It took an effort to handle the wheel-chair. With a cane in my hand and eyes blindfolded, I experienced myself walking in complete darkness. For me it was a five-minute walk, for a blind person, a lifetime. Sign language was also a challenge. I found out that sign language differs not only from country to country but from one region of country to another.

It was Arancha's idea to explain to children that some storybook and cartoon characters have disabilities: *Captain Hook* wears a big iron hook in place of his right hand (physical disability), which was eaten by a crocodile, who liked the taste so much that he follows Hook around constantly, hoping for more. *Dory*, a good-hearted and optimistic regal blue tang has short-term memory loss (intellectual disability) in the Disney film *Finding Nemo* while *Nemo*, a clownfish has a tiny right fin due to a minor injury to his egg, from a barracuda attack, which limits his swimming ability (physical disability). *The Three Blind Mice (Forder, Gorder, and Horder* from *Shrek)* are white mice that are blind and cannot see anything, and that's why they wear black sunglasses and carry cane (visual disability). *Hunchback of Notre Dame* depicts a person with a hunched back and misshapen face (physical disability).

Once Irene gave me a book *Chicken Soup for the Mother's Soul*, a 101 stories to open the hearts and rekindle the spirits of mothers. It is a book about mothers. I found for myself that not only in our culture do mothers cook chicken soup when their kids are sick. It is a universal notion which is composed of the following ingredients: chicken, broth, and lots of love.

In the book, there is a vignette written by Emily Perl Kingsley (a writer for the children's T.V. series *Sesame Street*), called "Welcome to Holland". It describes the feeling of a mother raising a child who has Down Syndrome. Irene knows every line of this story and I managed to translate it into Russian and Italian. Here it is in English:

I am often asked to describe the experience of raising a child with a disability –to try to help people who have not shared that unique experience to understand it, to imagine how it would feel. It's like this...

When you're going to have a baby, it's like planning a fabulous vacation trip –to Italy. You buy a bunch of guidebooks and make wonderful plans. The Coliseum. The Michelangelo David. The gondolas in Venice. You may learn some handy phrases in Italian. It's all very exciting.

After months of eager anticipation, the day finally arrives. You pack your bags and off you go. Several hours later, the plane lands. The stewardess comes and says, "Welcome to Holland".

"Holland?!" you say. "What do you mean, Holland?? I signed up for Italy! I'm supposed to be in Italy. All my life I've dreamed of going to Italy".

But there's been a change in the flight plan. They've landed in Holland and there you must stay.

The important thing is that they haven't taken you to a horrible, disgusting, filthy place, full of pestilence, famine and disease. It's just a different place.

So you must go and buy new guidebooks. And you must learn a whole new language. And you will meet a whole new group of people you would never have met.

It's just a different place. It's slower paced than Italy, less flashy than Italy. But after you've been there for a while and you catch your breath, you look around... and you begin to notice that Holland has windmills ...and Holland has tulips. Holland even has Rembrandts.

But everyone you know is busy coming and going from Italy... and they're all bragging about what a wonderful time they had there. And for the rest of your life, you will say, "Yes, that's where I was supposed to go. That's what I had planned".

And the pain of that will never, ever, ever, ever go away... because the loss of that dream is a very, very significant loss.

But...if you spend your life mourning the fact that you didn't get to Italy, you may never be free to enjoy the very special, the very lovely things...about Holland.

Much later Emily Pearl Kingsley published the continuation of her story:

I've been in Holland for more than a decade now. It has become my home. I've had time to regain my breath, to establish myself and make myself comfortable, and to accept something different to what I had planned.

Looking back, I reflect on the years when I had just arrived in Holland. I remember clearly the emotional blow, my fear, the pain and uncertainty. During these first years, I tried to come back to Italy, as I had planned, but in Holland was where I was supposed to remain. Today, I can say just how far I have gone on this unexpected trip. I've learned so much. But this path has taken its time.

I worked a lot. I bought new guidebooks. I learned a new language and slowly found my way in this new land. I met other people whose plans had changed, just like mine, and who could share my experience. We supported each other and some of them have become very special friends. Some of these travel companions had been in Holland much longer than me and they proved to be veteran guides, helping me during my travels. Many have encouraged me. Many have taught me to open my eyes to the wonders of this new land. I've discovered a community that is preoccupied. Holland is used to stray travelers, like me, and it has become a hospitable land, which extends its welcome hand, helps and supports newcomers like me.

During the years, I have asked myself how my life would have been had I landed in Italy, as planned. Would it have been easier? Would it have been as learned some of the most important lessons as I had in Holland? True, this trip has been more challenging and sometimes, I have stamped my feet and exclaimed in protest and frustration (I still do).

Indeed, Holland has a slower pace than Italy and it's less striking than Italy. But this has also turned into an unexpected advantage.

In a way, I've learned to slow down and look at things closer, gaining a new appreciation for Holland's beautiful things, with its tulips, windmills and works of Rembrandt.

I've come to love Holland and call it my home. I've become a world traveler and I've discovered that it does not matter where you land. What is more important is what you make of your trip, what you see and enjoy the special things, the beautiful things, the things of Holland or another land has to offer.

Indeed, it has been more than a decade since I arrived to a place I didn't plan on visiting. However, I am grateful, because this trip has been more enriching than I had ever imagined.

On October 22, 2011, I left for Alicante to attend a charity dinner organized by AODI. It was the sixth yearly event I was participating in, to meet friends and people raising children with disabilities, civic authorities, business people, sponsors, and volunteers. There were over 360 people, including the city mayor. It was almost the end of the evening when Matilde Diaz, the President of AODI, took the floor. She thanked everybody for coming and supporting the association, and she spoke about what had been done during the year and started talking about a woman who was a mother and a grandmother, without mentioning the name of the person. There was a silence in the air as everybody was guessing who it might be. Suddenly my photos taken at different times were displayed on the screen of the dinner hall. I saw my family, and myself, at receptions, meetings, at home. It was such a surprise for me that I didn't even realize it was all about me. Matilde called me a co-founder of the association, an active participant of AODI, and handed me an award in the form of a transparent plate with my name on it. For the first time the association established an award and it was decided unanimously by the board members to present it to me. For the first time in my life, abroad, I received gratitude from foreigners, from my favorite Spaniards. It was a great honor and inspiration for me!

The next day there was a motorcycle parade with 300 bikers from all over Spain, also organized by FLK to raise charity. Normally, we think of bikers as a wild bunch, maybe even violent, so it was a good way to eliminate another stereotype seeing a large group of bikers supporting a benefit for the people with disabilities. At one point, Irene asked everybody to stay in one place to take a photo for the media. I pushed Lucas's wheelchair forward and some bikers followed us to take their places around Lucas and me. Some of them sat in front of us on the ground. Since there were too many people for the photo, Irene asked everybody to get closer to each other and to move forward. I was going to push the wheelchair when I saw a biker right in front of us. I called him but he didn't hear me. People next to me started calling him too but he didn't hear us. And then Lucas, who seemed to have no interest in anything around him, who didn't talk, kicked the biker all of a sudden and Lucas turned his head to me as if trying to tell me: "Look, I got his attention!" I have known Lucas since he was two years old and I always thought he was indifferent, as he didn't understand what people told him, and so I was amazed to see his reaction. When Irene came up to us, I told her about Lucas. I saw tears in her eyes — she knew her son was able to react, so she was not surprised, just overjoyed. And I realized that nothing was in vain.

What I learned from the people with disabilities is that, in one way or another, we are all disabled, but we are all fortunate. Irene's severely disabled son Lucas has been fortunate not only in the family he has, but also in giving his name to a foundation and in that way inspiring work to make the world a better place to live. In his case, charity began at home, and is reaching far beyond.

Although at times I have felt swept away by a diplomatic tornado and overwhelmed by the constantly shifting challenges of multiculturalism, I have come to understand how truly fortunate I have been to live, in a certain way, a privileged life, sometimes even a fairytale. Like Dorothy, in *The Wizard of Oz*, I have learned that there is no place like home, though I have also learned that home is where you hang your hat. My life abroad has taught me to have more courage, like the lion, to think more carefully, like the scarecrow, and to have more heart, like the tin man. There may be wickedness in the world, but there is a lot of good, also, and we don't need a false wizard to teach us this. All we need is the magical example of the disabled, who inspire our courage, thoughtfulness, and compassion by welcoming us to their world. The charity that begins at home is to realize how lucky we all are, and stir that sense of luckiness in others. When we live in a new culture, we may feel blind, deaf, and dumb, or be treated that way, if we don't know the customs or the language. And yet, this multiculturalism is a privilege, a richness, if we know how to use it as such. We all have our difficulties, but, finally, we all live a privileged life. We all wear the ruby slippers to return home whenever we wish, if we consider home to be the best of ourselves.

This book is meant to provide ruby slippers for all of us who feel culturally lost and away from home. That is, we can be happy anywhere, in any cultural mix, if we appreciate the universal qualities of humanity wherever we go. The world is our home and solidarity our hearth. This may be the real message behind the curtain of the wizard of Oz. It is certainly the message behind the silk curtain of Kazakhstan.

EPILOGUE

Belgium in fall is beautiful. Our garden is covered with oriental carpet: red, yellow, brown, green, gold autumn colors.

Pushkin's verses about autumn come into my mind:

> *A melancholy time! So charming to the eye!*
> *Your beauty in its parting pleases me –*
> *I love the lavish withering of nature,*
> *The gold and scarlet raiment of the woods,*
> *The crisp wind rustling o'er their threshold.*
> *The sky engulfed by tides of rippled gloom,*
> *The sun's scarce rays, approaching frosts,*
> *And gray-haired winter threatening from afar.*[5]

Having spent fourteen years in total in Spain and Italy with evergreen scenery, we missed our autumnand winter in Kazakhstan. To touch snow, we used to drive to the north of Italy. Brussels reminds us of Kazakhstan's low season with rain and sun, changeable and unpredictable.

---

[5] A.S.Pushkin. From the Ends to the Beginning. A Billingual Anthology of Russian Verse, Editors: Ilya Kutik and Andrew Wachtel, Northwestern University, Chicago, IL, USA

For the first time of all our moving around, in Belgium I didn't have an adaptation period. Am I used to travelling or am I getting old? We spent nineteen years abroad moving from one country to another, adjusting to the new environment, changing homes, learning languages, getting attached to the places we lived in and to the people we made contact with.

Our daughters grew up abroad, received western educations, and got married. Our grandchildren were born and spent their early childhood abroad too. My husband made great achievements; he is respected and known, kind and generous. It was not an easy path for all of us. There were concerns, expectations, worries, mid-life crisis, menopause with mood switches, longing and missing, despair, loss of loved ones. We live and learn. We stay true to ourselves with our beliefs and try to maintain a positive attitude. We were challenged and we took on challenges. We changed. We changed for good.

I don't feel myself miserable anymore as I did at the beginning of our nomadic life. I am more experienced. I learned a lot. I matured. I became more confident. I have friends around the world. I have a caring husband and children.

I am happy to do what I love to do. I am interested in almost everything around me. I am curious and active. I am always on move, busy, overwhelmed and full of ideas.

Another day started. Another experience.

Another challenge...

BIBLIOGRAPHY
AND SUGGESTED READING

1. Aitken, Jonathan. Kazakhstan. *Surprises and Stereotypes. After 20 years of Independence*, Continuum, Great Britain, 2012

2. Ames, Helen Wattley. *Spain is Different*, Intercultu- ral Press, Yarmouth, ME, USA, 1999

3. Bewes, Diccon. *Swiss Watching. Inside Europe's Landlocked Island*, Nicholas Breadley Publishing, London-Boston, 2010

4. Canfield, Jack, Mark Victor Hansen, Jennifer Read Hawthorne, Marci Shimoff. *Chicken Soup for the Mother's Soul. 101 Stories to Open the Hearts and Rekindle the Spirits of Mothers*, Deerfield Beach, FL, USA, 1997

5. Clinton, Hillary Rodham. *It Takes a Village and Other Lessons Children Teach Us*, Simon and Schuster, USA, 1996

6. Epstein, Alan. *As the Roman Do. An American Family's Italian Odyssey*, Perennial, USA, 2001

7. Fulghum, Robert. *All I Really Need to Know I Learned in Kindergarten. Uncommon Thoughts on Common Things*, IVY Books, NY, USA, 1988

8. Hardy, Rae. *Distaff Diplomacy. My Elegant Life as a Diplomat's Wife*, Trafford, Canada, 2001

9. Holm, Bill. *Coming Home Crazy. An Alphabet of China Essays*, Milkweed Editions, Minneapolis, MN, USA, 2000

10. Keenan, Brigid. *Diplomatic Baggage. The Adven- tures of a Trailing Spouse*, John Murray, Great Britain, 2005

11. Nouwen, Henri J.M.. *A Spirituality of Fundraising*, Upper Room Books, Nashville, TN, USA, 2010

12. Oertig-Davidson, Margaret. *Beyond Chocolate. Understanding Swiss culture*, Bergli Books, Basel, Switzerland, 2011

13. Pollock, David C., Ruth E. Van Reken. *Third Culture Kids. Growing Among Worlds*, Nicholas Breadley Publishing, Boston-London, 2009

14. Pushkin, A.S. *From the Ends to the Beginning. A Bilingual Anthology of Russian Verse*, ed.: Ilya Kutik and

Andrew Wachtel, Northwestern Univer- sity, Chicago, IL, USA

15. Salhani, Claude. *Islam without a Veil. Kazakhstan's Path of Moderation*, Potomac Books, Washington, D.C. USA, 2011

16. Severgnini, Beppe. *An Italian in America, BUR Saggi, Italy*, 1995

www.ingramcontent.com/pod-product-compliance
Lightning Source LLC
Chambersburg PA
CBHW021436080526
44588CB00009B/544